Perfected in Christ

Other Books by Thomas Holton

Alive in Christ
Cultivated in Christ

Perfected in Christ

THOMAS HOLTON

CFI
An imprint of Cedar Fort, Inc.
Springville, Utah

© 2023 Thomas Holton
All rights reserved.

No part of this book may be reproduced in any form whatsoever, whether by graphic, visual, electronic, film, microfilm, tape recording, or any other means, without prior written permission of the publisher, except in the case of brief passages embodied in critical reviews and articles.

This is not an official publication of The Church of Jesus Christ of Latter-day Saints. The opinions and views expressed herein belong solely to the author and do not necessarily represent the opinions or views of Cedar Fort, Inc. Permission for the use of sources, graphics, and photos is also solely the responsibility of the author.

Paperback ISBN 13: 978-1-4621-4594-2
Ebook ISBN 13: 978-1-4621-3137-2

Published by CFI, an imprint of Cedar Fort, Inc.
2373 W. 700 S., Suite 100, Springville, UT 84663
Distributed by Cedar Fort, Inc., www.cedarfort.com

Library of Congress Control Number: 2023911683

Cover design by Shawnda Craig
Cover design © 2023 Cedar Fort, Inc.
Edited and Typeset by Liz Kazandzhy

Printed in the United States of America

10 9 8 7 6 5 4 3 2 1

Printed on acid-free paper

I dedicate this book with love to all those who want to believe that perfection through Christ is possible.

I am very grateful to my wife Veronica for her support in encouraging me to write about our Redeemer. I sincerely thank my son Thomas for reading the book in its entirety and offering His valuable recommendations.

I express my sincere appreciation to all at Cedar Fort for their efforts in bringing this work to fruition.

Contents

Introduction 1
1 Choose Sublime Offerings. 9
2 Covenant to Obey, Sacrifice, and Become Consecrated 17
3 Render Holy Gifts. 31
4 Rely on Christ's Power. 43
5 Engage in Special Connections 57
6 Experience Great Loves. 73
7 Use Precious Belongings 81
8 Display Significant Tokens 91
9 Give Valued Possessions. 105
10 Show Noble Signs 117
11 Make Daring Promises 131
12 Have Lofty Expectations 145
13 Sense Prized Anticipations 159
14 Enter into the Fellowship of Christ 171
15 Minister to the Holy One 183
16 Fill the Eternal Measure of Our Creation 197
17 Become Perfect in Christ. 213
About the Author 232

Introduction

I love my Lord and Savior, Jesus Christ. He is the light, life, and hope of our world.

In my first book, *Alive in Christ*, I focused on the marvelous greatness of the Son of God. I highlighted the majestic newness of life that He can bring to each of us as we come unto Him with full purpose of heart. My hope was that our love, respect, and admiration for Him would continue to grow.

In my second book, *Cultivated in Christ*, I focused on how the Savior views each of us. His noble perspective of our destiny calls us to a higher life. My desire was that our love for ourselves would continue to be rooted in our deep love for Him.

I now turn my attention to the possibility of attaining *Perfection in Christ*, the title of this book. I have come to understand that such perfection is not only possible but also both feasible and inevitable as we truly come to live and grow and ultimately mature *in and through* Christ. We do not become perfect on our own. Perfection is relational. It requires mutual linking with the Son of God. The Book of Mormon teaches us that if you "come unto Christ, and [are] perfected *in him* . . . [and] love God with all your might, mind and strength, then is his grace sufficient for you, that *by his grace* ye may be perfect *in* Christ" (Moroni 10:32; emphasis added). In other words, perfection—which is wholeness, completeness, being finished or perfectly formed—is only possible through loyal connection with God. In my view, this connection is essentially tied up with covenant religion. In essence, the degree of our salvation depends on the extent of our covenant abiding in Christ. What I mean by this will become more apparent as we proceed.

In essence, the grace of Christ can only make us perfect if we learn to love God entirely. Without our keeping of sacred promises to God, even His grace is not enough to perfect us. Insofar as we refuse to do that which we can do, grace cannot cover us. Agency and grace are not contradictory. Grace works in accordance with our genuine desires, not against them. Hence, the final polishing of our souls to make them fully fit for heaven comes through welding ourselves with the Son of God. By this means, we are fully participative in the process and outcome of salvation. I hope to show how the idea of relational religion means that only when we come to relate to Christ like He relates to us will we find that we are participants in the kind of perfect salvation that He offers.

So the thrust of this book will be to suggest the following: that the preconditions for perfection are that we need to experience the kind of covenant union with Christ that He offers to us. Therefore, I will focus on our capacity to give of our deepest selves to Him—to make precious offerings to Him of that which is most dear to us. Obviously, the great gifts He has given us then become the valued gifts we offer back to Him, except they are now multiplied greatly in both scope and scale. Hence, there is a union of feeling and devotion between us and Christ that is both deep and everlasting. This is the true nature of perfection. As true communication requires more than one communicator, so true perfection requires holy partnership.

I want to paint a picture of what we bring to the table, what we can offer at the altar, and what we can make available for His service. We each have gifts, whether they be artistic, musical, literary, or athletic. We each have capabilities—physically, intellectually, emotionally, and spiritually. In my view, the most vital "gift" or "talent" of all is the ability to discern and hearken to the voice of God, to recognize spiritual realities, to cultivate mastery over the crude elements of our nature, and to craft a life of deep and abiding connection to God. This is a talent we can develop, increase, and improve if we seek it, ask for it, make room for it, and work at it. Hence, I place a premium on developing the primary "gift" of spirituality. Of course, all aspects of our being are made better through association with the Son of God. He refines every gift we possess, every ability we acquire. He improves every worthwhile value and every enjoyable skill.

My encouragement is for us to continue to serve others based on our divine love for our Lord. When we reach the point of reciprocity with the Lord, in that we relate to Him as He does to us, then we find a new kind of alignment. When our connection with Him becomes rock solid and our bond is one of mutual love and respect, then we have found joy supernal. Thus, this book will concentrate primarily on what we become willing to do—for Christ and for others—so that we might truly be one in Him, refined in Him, beloved in Him. In other words, that we might become perfected *in* Him as He is perfected in and through the Father.

What Shall We Give?

I love the story of the wise men. Each traveled far. Each brought a gift they felt was worthy of the greatest King the world would ever see. The nobility of their offering was not just in the material treasure presented; more importantly, it was in the nobility of soul that accompanied their gift. The gold represents the best of our selves, the frankincense indicates the prayers that ascend to heaven, and the myrrh shows that bitterness can become sweet healing.

These wise men—and each of these precious gifts—has given us an example to follow, a type to teach us, and a lesson to learn. In the scriptures, wisdom is usually correlated with obedience to God and hearing His instruction. These wise men were men seeking to obey the voice of God, to know the guidance of the Almighty.

If you had been one of the wise men, consider these questions:

- What distance would you have traveled to see the Christ child?
- What personal gift would you have brought to the precious child?
- What thoughts would you have had upon seeing the new star?
- What feelings would you have felt on seeing His sweet face?
- What memories would you have carried within you of that special encounter?
- What truths would you have shared with others about this most profound event?

A beloved hymn teaches us about our opportunity to give something rare to Christ:

> What shall *we give* to the Babe in the manger?
> What shall *we offer* the Child in the stall?
> Incense and spices and gold we've aplenty,
> Are these the gifts for the King of us all?
>
> What shall *we give* to the Boy in the temple?
> What shall *we offer* the Man by the sea?
> Palms at His feet and hosannas uprising,
> Are these for Him who will carry the tree?
>
> What shall *we give* to the Lamb who was offered,
> Rising the third day and shedding His love?
> Tears for His mercy *we'll weep* at the manger,
> *Bathing* the infant come down from above.[1]

Who gave offerings to the King Jesus, and what gifts did they give Him? Let us ponder this:

- Mary gave birth to and nourished Him.
- Joseph trained and provided for Him.
- Mary (the sister of Lazarus) washed His feet with oil and tears.

---

1. Ashley Dewey, "What Shall We Give To The Babe In The Manger," LDS Blogs, Dec. 25, 2016, https://ldsblogs.com/35260/shall-give-babe-manger; emphasis added.

- A leper expressed gratitude for healing.
- A blind man thanked and witnessed of Him.
- A man prepared the upper room for Him for the Last Supper.
- An angel comforted Him in Gethsemane.

Many other examples could be offered. I am struck by the range of gifts He received—everything from bodily life to practical knowledge to tenderness, respect, and compassion. He was given food, water, clothing, and shelter. He had friends. People gave Him attention, time, resources, and association. They gave Him things He needed in the moment and expressions of gratitude and devotion. Obviously, the Savior was a servant and He was primarily here in mortality to serve others. However, He was also served. He was noticed, watched, and observed—not only by those who were suspicious of Him but especially by those who wanted to know Him and help Him. This helps us to see that the possessions we have can indeed be useful as gifts to God. Whether these belongings are physical or spiritual, the giving of them to God to support His cause and build His kingdom is worthwhile. In addition, the gifts we give to bless others are also like an offering to God: "And the King shall answer and say unto them, Verily I say unto you, Inasmuch as ye have done it unto one of the least of these my brethren, ye have done it unto me" (Matthew 25:40).

I have long been convinced that each of us is on a journey of giving. We have precious presents to offer to God that only we can give. So often this giving is reflected in what we offer to the other travelers around us in this desert wilderness of a weary world. These gifts—of all that we possess and are—represent the most important offerings in time and eternity. As we come to see the great gifts that God has given us—both material and spiritual—we will want to bless others by showering gifts upon them to aid them in their journey toward life eternal.

In terms of temporal giving, we are instructed that even if we are poor in temporal things, we should only deny the beggar if we do not have resources to offer. In essence, our desire is to be one of saying "if I had I would give" (Mosiah 4:24). In other words, our wish is to be of assistance. The Lord warns the temporally rich who will not assist the poor by means of material substance that "riches will canker your souls; and this shall be your lamentation in the day of visitation, and of judgment, and of indignation: The harvest is past, the summer is ended, and my soul is not saved!" (Doctrine and Covenants 56:16). In essence, if the desire for riches overrides the desire to help others in need, then our own spiritual salvation is at risk. God has instructed us that "unto whom much is given much is required" (Doctrine and Covenants 82:3). Thus, if we receive any form of abundance from God, He requires us to do a commensurate amount of good with it.

Modern revelation teaches us that our moral imperative is to be actively involved in the cause of goodness. We are to voluntarily choose to do many things that are of much good: "Verily I say, men should be anxiously engaged in a good cause, and *do many things* of their own free will, and bring to pass much righteousness; For *the power is in them*, wherein they are agents unto themselves. And inasmuch as men do good they shall in nowise lose their reward" (Doctrine and Covenants 58:27–28; emphasis added).

We are taught that we have power to do many great and valuable things. This is a doctrine of taking initiative, showing creativity, being intentional, and using our inherent capacity to make righteous things happen. I love that this is placed within our grasp. God expects us to be planning and preparing to do good, to be up and doing, and to succeed in our godly labors. To bring to pass these things is to perform them, accomplish them, and make them real. The fact that this service is a free will offering makes it more special and potent.

Every child of God has unique and wonderful gifts to offer to God and their fellow mortals. As we discover these gifts and share them with the world, we are glorifying God. We are also blessing the lives of those our lives touch either directly or indirectly. Our influence makes a difference. Our gifts are needed. Our offerings have merit. I invite each one of us to consider what lies within us—some of which is presently undiscovered—which we might bring forth and lay on the altar of the Lord. As we come to sense this reality, we will know and experience that abundant joy of using our gifts in Christlike ways. Our life will become more of a beautiful offering to God.

I am therefore convinced that perfection in and through Christ is possible. I believe this perfection comes only when we come to love Him as He loves us, only as we come to serve Him as He serves us, only when we come to offer to Him all that we have and are. We become like Him, perfect like He already is. This book is my heartfelt and reasoned explanation about how such perfection is indeed possible. Let us rejoice in the adventure of reaching our ultimate perfection in Christ.

1
Choose Sublime Offerings

The potential for creative excellence resides within each of us, and it is vital that we detect and develop this potential. By sensing the divinity of our capacities, we are positioned to offer a truly great gift to God. I also believe we can offer the greatest gifts to God by discovering the things we are most divinely inspired in. There are many unique creative gifts we can offer to God, and we do so by developing them and showcasing them to the glory of God and the blessing of His children.

I believe in the grand design of creation. When I look to the heavens, I am stunned by the scope and scale of our galaxy. Likewise, when I look at the mountains, valleys, rivers, lakes, trees, and flowers, I think of the essential beauty of creation. I see the hand of God in the purpose and design of this material world. The beauty of this earth is patterned after the much greater loveliness of heaven. I love to see creations that reflect God's glory, whether physical or artistic. I also see God's goodness in the creative capacities of our lives. Our ability to bring lovely form out of chaos stems from the divine spark within us. We are not brought into being for a fleeting moment only. We are participants in a magnificent design.

I am convinced that excellence, in its pure and pristine form, is evidence of divinity. The marvelous endowments that have been expressed culturally on this earth are reflections of the gifted excellence of God. Consider the following:

- The excellence of writing reflected in Herman Melville's *Moby Dick*
- The musical praise of George Frideric Handel's *Messiah*
- The message of Martin Luther King's "I Have a Dream" speech
- The beauty in Sir Isaac Newton's theology and mathematics
- The linguistic abilities of William Tyndale and his love for God's word
- The breathtaking scope of John Milton's epic poem "Paradise Lost"
- The sculpting capacity shown in Michelangelo's statue of David
- The astonishing architecture of Sir Christopher Wren's St. Paul's Cathedral

Certainly, something valuable would have been lost if these persons had never "created" these great works. We would be poorer musically, scientifically, and artistically if such persons had not lived or if they had not pursued their great gifts in earnest. It is not simply that their works represent supreme achievements culturally and intellectually. Nor is it just the emotions they evoke, the ideas they share, and the profundities they embody. It is not even the fact that these works carry an almost timeless quality. It is the reality that they are, in at least some measure, inspired. They are gifts from a divine source. They go beyond the normal and mundane. They reach beyond the routine of everyday life and portray, to some degree, the glory and handiwork of God. They are hints at His magnificence, reflections of His beauty, intimations of His power, and testimonies of His grandeur. I believe each one of these works would have been impossible in the absence of a portion of divine intervention. The creators had a portion of the Light of Christ, which gave them some spiritual and moral genius.

I love both revelation-based inspiration and the fields of human knowledge. I see no fundamental incongruity between the truths of revealed religion and the laws of material reality. In verity, I see a beautiful harmony between the physical and spiritual, mind and matter, and time and eternity. God is the author of law, including the laws which provide for the miracles of creation and resurrection, the order of solar systems, the beauty of photosynthesis, the power of gravity, the mechanics of engines, the wonder of music, the awe of art, and the majesty of literature, to name but a few. One day, we will be able to comprehend this unity far better than we do now. I fully agree with Alma that "all things denote that there is a Supreme Creator" (Alma 30:44).

But these marvelous endowments from God don't stop there. They are reflected in every area of life. Consider the capabilities of those who use their gifts in their everyday lives:

- Doctors who remember and heal
- Accountants who count and categorize
- Lawyers who distinguish and articulate
- Architects who imagine and design
- Engineers who envision and craft
- Teachers who explain and guide

Lest we think these privileges are limited to those of superb IQ or noble birth, we are well-advised to remember that the gifts of divinity have been given to every person. As we reflect on our lives, seek the opinions of those around us, and experiment with the gifts God has given us (including those we are yet unaware of), then we come to see that each child of God has gifts that are godly in nature, albeit in elementary form. What is the purpose of these abilities? It is for the glory of God and the furtherance of His majestic purposes. It is for the advancement of joy, peace, meaning, and hope among all. It is to bless each and every life.

Uncover the Divine

It is only incrementally that we come to discover the true character of God, truth, creation, intelligence, and ourselves. These discoveries take time, experience, effort, and patience. God reveals our true nature, identity, gifts, abilities, and potential to us through a series of unveilings. We are gradually able to sense who we are and who others are only through a line-upon-line process. This is the process of divine uncovering. When Alma encourages us to have the image of God engraven upon our countenances (see Alma 5), he is speaking both of a one-time experience and an ongoing reality. *Emmanuel* means "God with us," and we are to come to see—by degrees—that He truly is. God is also in us, but not in some strange, supernatural way. Rather, it is in the sense that through divine revelation and artistic inspiration, we come to see our godlike abilities and those of others.

There are parts of ourselves we have not yet discovered. There are elements of our potentiality that are still to become known, enlarged upon, and brought to full development. We are being renewed regularly in our understanding of things divine. As we catch hold upon this thought, we come to sense security, strength, and exhilaration in the ideas this uncovering brings to light. We are all bound by temporary constraints and limited by various temporal and spiritual restrictions. As we come to Christ, He eases our burdens and makes us greater than before. When Christ ministers to us, He activates this process of uncovering so that we can see all things better. When Paul refers to "[seeing] through a glass, darkly" (1 Corinthians 13:12), part of what he could mean is that we see God, ourselves, and others with a blurred perspective in this mortal life. As truth becomes more visible to us, we eventually come to see as we are seen and know as we are known.

It is a great adventure to ask and answer the following kinds of questions:

- What truths can I yet learn?
- What gifts can I yet receive?
- What abilities can I soon acquire?

- What knowledge can I someday obtain?
- What wisdom can I still develop?

The truth is given to us by God. We all benefit from understanding divine truth and comprehending the reality that we can continually grow into someone more divine. Coming to discern truth, goodness, and beauty in ourselves and others is vital if we are to offer to God the precious contribution that only we can make.

Harness the Creative Power of God's Word

There is real virtue (power) in the word of God. By the power of God's remarkable words, tremendous works are made manifest. His words formed and changed the world. If we allow it, God's word can be far more powerful than any other force in our lives. Divine words are creative, life-giving, spectacular, wondrous, amazing, miraculous, and deeply powerful. The words we learn, know, and speak matter. They can contribute to glorious plans and purposes—if they are God's good words! Indeed, by learning the words of God, we are empowered to do things that would otherwise be impossible. We can come to use words in the way God uses them and thereby come to do great work in His cause. We can bless others through the words we speak—words of comfort, consolation, uplift, warning, encouragement, nourishing, and hope. What words spoken to you by others have bolstered your belief in your capacity to do and be good? It is likely that such words have impacted you greatly for good!

Unlock Our Desire to Create

The gospel of God is in truth the ultimate message of magnificent purpose. It envisions something far grander for us than we imagine. In this world, our perspective is often limited by mortal horizons, by difficult circumstances, and by confining attitudes. God seeks to open our eyes, unlock our latent capacity, and increase our expectation. The power to create resides within our divine DNA. We have a longing for the eternal, an intense desire for the beautiful, and a deep interest in the overarching searching of the soul.

If we are impressed by human achievements in art, science, music, literature, dance, photography, technology, athletics, and other areas in which humans excel, then what might we feel if we were fully introduced to the capabilities of angels and gods? If our creative capacities were improved beyond the confines of mortal constraints, we would be enabled to do better in all these areas. I marvel at our imaginative ingenuity, our venturing forth into previously undiscovered terrain, and our ability to capture that which is beautiful in a moment of time. I am constantly impressed by the amazing achievements in all fields of human endeavor. I believe that without our divine origin, such accomplishments would not be possible. I also sense that it is only as we come to see our nature in divine terms that we can bring to full fruition our creative potential in every area.

Unleash the Power of Creation

God is the ultimate creative genius. He has performed His creative acts in such a way that we are incorporated into His plans and purposes. We are "touched" by His light-filled life. We are moved, energized, and sparked to newness. We "see" something that we are amazed by, drawn to, and electrified through. God is magnetic, attractive, and revitalizing. His influence is shocking, enlivening, and emboldening. He wakes us up from a slumber of complacency, boredom, frustration, and inaction.

God is a relational being. We come from Him, connect with Him, and long for Him. He has gifted us with His divine capacities in a rudimentary but also powerful form. His intelligence is such that it inevitably reveals itself throughout creation. Our capacity reflects His. Our greatness stems from His mighty power. Our ability with language, mathematics, art, science, and everything else mirrors His phenomenal nature. He shares His power with us. We see His goodness, love, courage, and a thousand other attributes of His nature being manifest in and through us. We are something of the living embodiment of His creative sharing.

As we come to know that we are His, we are empowered to unleash our creative gifts in ways that will bless the world, in a manner that will ignite the spark for greatness in others. Every wonderful gift, every holy trait, every precious talent, every worthwhile endeavor—these are all the inheritance of Almighty God to His children. It is therefore our special privilege to exercise our gifts in godlike ways. It is also essential that our gifts be used in such a way that they benefit and bless others. We relay permission, sanction, and excitement to others as we use our God-granted endowments in the cause of generating more light, greater hope, additional love, increased faith, and enhanced joy in this world.

When we see God as our Father who gifts us with His precious powers, we want to be close to Him. We want to be with Him and be like Him. Also, we want to use our influence to invite and encourage others to draw close to Him. Our words are then used to ignite the spark of faith in others. Our gifts are directed toward inspiring others to seek their own gifts for the glory of God. Our talents are used to enrich the lives of our fellow beings.

We are all co-creators with God. We create many things in this world. We have the innate capacity to be a light to others, a source of encouragement, a beacon for growth. When we turn our attention to that which truly adds value, to that which magnifies the good, to that which generates creativity, to that which endorses generosity, and to that which promotes the sharing of our energies in positive ways, then we are in touch with our creative destiny. We are living the way God designed us to live—as giving, sharing, serving, productive creators.

Creation is a moving force by its very nature. Creation is electrifying. It is the process of multiplicity through power. Creation is not a stale, boring, dry event. It is a transfer of energy, a migration of potentiality. Kinetic creation provides metaphorical light and heat. God moves in and through us. Whether we desire to excel in academic pursuits, artistic efforts, literary endeavors, talent competitions, administrative roles, protective tasks, or leadership functions, we are most successful when we use the divine power of God to optimal effect. This power infuses the world with glory, truth, enlightenment, and happiness. Creation grounded in God is magnificent, purposeful, and triumphant.

A creator does not just use their own power to make exciting things happen—they induct the minds, hearts, spirits, and bodies of others into the cause. A wise person does not simply use the power of their own mind or body to accomplish creative outflow. Rather, they engage the creative spark to ignite the minds and bodies of others in service of the generation of new and beautiful things. When we see others using imagination to turn concepts into actuality, we are beckoned to do likewise. Music begets more music, poetry inspires further poetry, love encourages additional love, and so on. It is a domino effect. Ideas catch fire by being relayed with enthusiasm from one person to another. They spread contagiously. When one person uses their creative gift well, it ignites a sense of vision for others to do likewise.

Great encouragement comes when others teach us how to flourish. For example, when a talented performer showcases their skills to the world, others are influenced to do likewise. The "magic" of excellence rubs off on us. It educates us in terms of what is achievable. It invites us to do and be more. It affects us profoundly as we are inspired and motivated to change our perception of what might be done in our own lives and in the world around us. This influential force of creation transmits a potent capacity to us. We are enlivened by witnessing such flowing creative power.

In conclusion, our most sublime offerings to God are those that represent the best we have to offer. As we seek God first in our lives, He makes us into better versions of ourselves. His words and creative abilities transform us into creative beings. Let us dig deep and reach high in offering the best of ourselves to God.

2

Covenant to Obey, Sacrifice, and Become Consecrated

Covenants present us with unique opportunities to offer very specific types of gifts to God. Does the restored gospel of Jesus Christ provide us with a greater understanding of our possibilities, including what our relationships can be like? I answer with a resounding yes! Are there spiritual blessings that come to us only as we make and keep sacred covenants? I believe there surely are. I am assured that God has given us access to covenants so that we can become something more than we could be without them. As we become more, we can offer more. In this sense, there are gifts we can offer to God and our fellow men and women by entering sacred covenants that we could not otherwise offer. Let us examine the nature of revealed religion, the essentials of sacrifice, the essence of covenants, and the fundamentals of how our offerings to the Lord are in token of Christ's great atoning sacrifice. These are things we must know and do if we are to become perfect in Christ.

Awake and Arise to the Need for Covenant Religion

An angel of God visited King Benjamin during the night to give him a vital message. He instructed the king to "awake" (Mosiah 3:2) to the joyful message of Christ's coming to the earth in a future day to bring atoning salvation to the world. This truth was to bring tremendous rejoicing both to the prophet-king and his people (see Mosiah 3:2–4). The people of King Benjamin did find great joy in this message. They began to understand the importance of entering into covenants of obedience with God:

> And we are *willing to enter into a covenant* with our God to do his will, and to be obedient to his commandments in all things that he shall command us, all the remainder of our days, that we may not bring upon ourselves a never-ending torment, as has been spoken by the angel, that we may not drink out of the cup of the wrath of God.
>
> And now, these are the words which king Benjamin desired of them; and therefore he said unto them: Ye have spoken the words that I desired; and the covenant which ye have made is a *righteous covenant*.
>
> And now, because of the covenant which ye have made ye shall be called the children of Christ, his sons, and his daughters; for behold, this day he hath spiritually begotten you; for ye say that your hearts are changed through faith on his name; therefore, ye are born of him and have become his sons and his daughters. (Mosiah 5:5–7; emphasis added)

It is evident that the king's people were so enlightened, inspired, encouraged, and transformed by this heavenly message that they responded with a willingness to make and keep a covenant of righteousness that would be for all the days of their lives. In essence, the people *wanted* to do God's will. They did not resist Him. They desired to escape the bondage of sin and death. Hence, they made a covenant that was righteous. They did the right thing, the appropriate thing, the good thing! Thus, they became spiritually related to Christ as new children of Him. They would be joint heirs with Christ on conditions of obedience and repentance throughout life.

We likewise can be yoked by covenant to God (see John 15:5–11). We are covenant Christians. God offers His covenant to each of us to bring us to a loving, permanent relationship with Him. This vital truth can be understood, felt, appreciated, embraced, lived, and shared by us individually. Our relationship with God works better when we choose to engage with Him. He invites us to join with Him by covenant—by mutual consent. Indeed, this doctrine of choosing is especially important to the idea of covenants. We *choose* to enter covenants, to engage in sacred agreements. There is no compulsion to do so. It is anticipated that having used our own voluntary decision-making capacities to partake in covenants with God, we will strive to be faithful to our promises. This is the foundation of all significant progress in matters of spirituality.

To be bound to God by covenant is an eternally significant responsibility. Consequently, the blessings pertaining to covenant faithfulness far surpass any other possible rewards in time and eternity. God honors our choice to follow Him with opportunities that are amazing in scope and scale. When we come to understand and appreciate what the Father and Son have done for us, our hearts and minds are moved to offer ourselves to their great cause. We are not simply spectators but are participants in the great work of salvation. True religion and spirituality always involve the giving of our most precious gifts in loyalty to our most cherished causes.

If kings and prophets need to awake and arise to divine messages, then surely we need to do the same. Each one of us is being called to "awake and arise" to God's great revelations. Whether by means of the conscience-promoting light of Christ, the soul-piercing invitations of the Holy Ghost, the action-commanding voice of holy angels, or the very voice of God Himself, we are being instructed to become alert and attentive to the truths of heaven. We are to listen carefully and to focus intently on these inspirational messages God has for us. These communications center in the Son of God, in covenant loyalty, in the call to be up and doing, in the solemn warnings to repent, and in the opportunity to rejoice in God's goodness. We each have a work to do in these last days. Now is the time to be about our Father's business in gathering ourselves and others to the new and everlasting covenant restored in our day through Joseph Smith.

Welcome First Principles, Primary Ordinances, and Foundational Covenants

As part of the Restoration, we are given the primary principle of faith in the Lord Jesus Christ. Acceptance of His divine sonship is at the core of our belief system. This is a first truth because it forms the solid basis of that which follows it. It is not something we can truthfully regard as trivial, unimportant, optional, or secondary. It empowers, sustains, renews, and informs every aspect of what we value. His unique power over sin and death makes Him special. True faith in Him is powerful. It leads to us forsaking the low road of life and inclining ourselves toward greatness of character. True faith and repentance in Christ always lead to engagement in ordinances and covenants. These ceremonial practices are deeply significant. They show in bodily form what we long for spiritually. They enact our faith at the level of practical reality. These are authorized rituals that carry great implication. They are means of us accessing divine knowledge, understanding, power, and protection. As Jacob saw in vision a ladder that stretched to heaven, so the ordinances of the gospel order connect us to God in both time and eternity. Glory comes from ascending the covenant steps of righteousness.

Know the True Nature of Covenant Sacrifice

Let us consider the deep substance of the greatest sacrifice of all—the offering of the Lamb without blemish (see 1 Peter 1:18–20; Doctrine and Covenants 138:2; Moses 7:47). Christ is the sacrificial offering given in our behalf. Such an offering was:

- Holy—It was done by a being without sin. "Worthy is the Lamb that was slain" (Revelation 5:12).

- Pure—It was given with sublime motive. Christ had no part in giving any wicked, impure, unholy, or inappropriate offerings to His Father.
- Without broken bones—It was done in fulfillment of prophecy.
- That of the Firstborn—It was an example all others could respect. The Lamb of God is the Son of the Eternal Father and the Savior of the world (see 1 Nephi 13:40; 1 Nephi 11:21).
- Without opening His mouth—It was made without complaint or protest. "He is brought as a lamb to the slaughter" (Isaiah 53:7; see also Mosiah 14:7).
- Redemptive in its consequence for those who believe in Christ—We are to look to the Lamb of God because He takes away the sin of the world (see John 1:29; Alma 7:14). Our stained garments are made white in the blood of the Lamb because of our faith in Him (see 1 Nephi 12:11). We are to cry mightily unto the Father in the name of Jesus, that we may be cleansed by the blood of the Lamb (see Mormon 9:6; Revelation 7:14; Alma 34:36). We overcome Satan by the blood of the Lamb (see Revelation 12:11).

The Atonement of Christ was far more than an animal sacrifice or human sacrifice could ever be. It was necessary that it be a great and last sacrifice (see Alma 34:10). It could not be a small sacrifice or a first sacrifice. It had to be the most significant, difficult, costly, and demanding of all sacrifices. It was the ultimate sacrifice in that nothing else could be more magnanimous. No animal or human could make such an offering. It was infinite and eternal. Hence, its reach would extend forever. His was the sacrifice of an eternal being (see Alma 34:11–12). Human sacrifices can only meet human demands or human crimes. Only the offering of a divine life could cover the sins of humans without simultaneously demanding that those humans die for their sins.

It is sobering that His was a culminating sacrifice (see Alma 34:13). The Atonement allowed for animal sacrifice to be done away with because there was no need for animal blood to be shed after the blood of God's Son was already shed. (Indeed, to shed animal blood after Christ had died would perhaps have been a mockery before God akin to infant baptism, unless Christ commanded it in special remembrance of Him, such as when He comes again.) Christ fulfilled the law of Moses with total perfection. It was a pinnacle sacrifice (see Alma 34:14). All other sacrifices point to this ultimate one—the sacrifice of God's Only Begotten Son. It was a sacrifice that brings salvation to believers (see Alma 34:15). Thus, mercy overpowers justice so that people can have faith in Christ unto the repentance and forgiveness of their sins.

Christ can indeed transform our life from one of crimson-red sin to white-as-snow righteousness. The Lord, through the seer Isaiah, said, "Come now, and let us reason together, saith the Lord: though your sins be as scarlet, they shall be as white as snow; though they be red like crimson, they shall be as wool" (Isaiah 1:18). This promise still applies in these last days. As the blood-stained clothing of Christ was replaced by white garments after His Resurrection, so too He can overcome the stain, decay, and death inherent in our sin as we come sincerely to Him. Our clothing of crimson-scarlet sins will be replaced, on conditions of sincere repentance, by the white wool that will warm, comfort, and protect us. Like clean white snow, our very lives will become fresh, new, clean, vibrant, and beautiful. This is the very miracle of forgiveness that Christ promises to those who come to rely on His atoning blood with loyalty and regularity.

It is my conviction that Christ agreed to atone by means of covenant. His was a covenant offering. Such a voluntary but binding obligation carries a weight and a reward that far exceeds an offering made without covenant responsibility or resolve. When our offerings are made in similitude of His ultimate offering, they are truly something worth giving to God.

Comprehend the Covenant Blessings of Sacrifice

Adam and Eve made sacrificial offerings to the Lord in representation of the sacrifice of God. Their offering of the firstlings of their flocks resembled the sacrifice of the Only Begotten of the Father (see Moses 5:5–8). This was to be a pattern followed by their children. It is a great blessing for us to understand that Christ redeems us from sin and death. It is only by our performing sacrifices as commanded by God that we bring His atoning sacrifice to remembrance often. Animal sacrifices were a type of God's offering of Himself. In due course, the form of the offering would change from being one of a precious animal to being one of our own hearts and spirits.

Jesus offered *Himself* as a sacrifice for sin (see 2 Nephi 2:6–7). He who was filled with truth and divine aid was willing to show His love for His Father and for us by giving His all to us. To make amends for broken spiritual laws, He paid the price so that lawbreakers (the rest of us) could be reconciled to God the Father. We know that our redemption required His atoning act. It also requires that we offer a broken heart and a contrite spirit to God (see 3 Nephi 9:20). God wants us to give our innermost selves to Him. There is in this truth a reciprocity of sacrifice. All must make sacrifices if they seek to become one with God. Sacrifice is essential to salvation. Therefore, redemption comes through the atoning sacrifice of Jesus Christ to those who are *willing to sacrifice*. Hence, His sacrifice leads us to making our own sacrifices in His name and in His cause. Indeed, both the living and the dead are taught about Christ's sacrifice and how they need to make sacrifices themselves as a type of Christ: "And so it was made known among the dead, both small and great, the unrighteous as well as the faithful, that redemption had been wrought *through the sacrifice of the Son of God upon the cross*" (Doctrine and Covenants 138:35; emphasis added).

What gifts did prophets offer in sacrifice to the divine cause? Adam gave his choicest flocks. Enoch gave his fears. Noah relinquished his reputation. Abraham offered his precious son. Moses surrendered his status. Peter submitted his energy and passion. Joseph Smith yielded up his comforts and convenience. Those who truly love Christ are willing to offer Him *everything in this life*. Those who sacrifice in true token of Christ also experience tribulation in His name (see Doctrine and Covenants 138:13). We ought not to expect that living in the right way will be unopposed, easy, blissful, tranquil, safe, or comfortable all the time. We are expected to withstand a measure of difficulty.

Offer an Acceptable Covenant Sacrifice

Sacrifice brings forth the holy in us. It costs us something. It evidences our devotion to God. Sacrifice must be representative of what the Father and the Son offered in order to save us. They gave of Themselves. To be a worthy sacrifice, the offering must remind us of the Son of God. A "holy" offering is a sacred one made by a holy person in a specially designated way. We imitate, at least to some degree, what the Father and Son did in giving an offering that is worthy to be called such. This is why the scriptures speak about us keeping our covenants by an *acceptable* sacrifice.

We witness our devotion to God by our willingness to sacrifice. The Anti-Nephi-Lehies buried their weapons of war for the sake of peace. This represented a stark departure from a prolonged previous way of life. This was a true sign of a sincere desire to follow the Prince of Peace. Those who gave burnt offerings of precious livestock surely made a genuine attempt to please God. Otherwise, the animals would have been used for food or sold to make money. Fast offerings show generosity so that others can be blessed. This is putting our faith into action. It literally costs us both money and calories (energy) to give that which we might have retained to ourselves. Free will offerings involve giving that which no one has compelled us to give. Such is a token of voluntary love. It is an act made sacred because it originates within the innermost part of our souls.

Let us ponder the meaning of our most holy offerings:

- Did the twelve-year-old boys who brought lambs to the temple for an offering consider the sufferings of that lamb they carried to pay their debt in symbolic fashion?
- Do I ponder the thoughts, feelings, and sufferings of the Lamb of God in His messianic offering?
- Am I sensitive to what my salvation really cost?

- Are my offerings given in resemblance, token, and reminder of what the Father and Son offered the world?

Let us also remember that sacrifices can consist of small offerings. If they are given in the right spirit, the small yet significant contributions of good people are an acceptable offering to God.

Serve with Loyalty to Covenant

God calls people to His holy work in this age. Through the spirit of prophecy and revelation, individuals are selected by God to become prophets, seers, and revelators. They are chosen to accept the burden of leadership, to be an example to the world of what living a godly life looks like. They teach God's doctrines, promote His purposes, perform His ordinances, safeguard His scriptures, offer His covenants, convey His power, and bestow His blessings upon others. God is intervening in this world through His designated servants. Following the prophet is not an act of blind faith; rather, it is an act of inspired vision.

In addition, God prepares each one of us in smaller but still important ways—as we hear His voice and follow His direction—to be called to serve, asked to lead, and invited to bless. There is law and order in how God performs and accomplishes His plans. We can know that those called by God will also be strengthened by Him as they are humble and prayerful. This includes us in our small arenas of loving service. I believe that sacrifices of our time and talents in the cause of Christ are very important to our salvation. It is by giving ourselves in these ways that we find that such service matters to God. Service we give out of covenant loyalty is much stronger than service we give because we are simply called. Being called is important. However, being devoted to covenants primarily means that our service is strongly anchored in relationship to God. Our efforts are then more likely to be rooted in loving communion and loyalty.

Bind Ourselves to God's Covenant Institution

God has a Church that He calls His own. As a God of law and order, He is interested in ordinances, ordinations, and organizations. Through the Prophet Joseph Smith, God has restored His divinely authorized and empowered kingdom to the earth. This gospel kingdom is patterned after that which existed in heavenly realms. It mirrors that which operated under divine sanction in Old and New Testament times. The Church of God must bear His name, commission His duly constituted officers, perform His sacraments, preach His doctrines, teach His plans, reveal His covenants, sustain His commandments, communicate His revelations, empower His people, and bless His children. The Church of Jesus Christ of Latter-day Saints embodies these principles and practices with marvelous clarity and impact. It is organization of the best and highest kind.

I believe God has given us a true and living Church. God promotes not simply generic goodness but organized righteousness. He values truth, ordinances, and covenants rather than chance, chaos, and casualness. He desires to give us a clear means for dispensing His doctrines, knowing His laws, obtaining His mysteries, receiving His rituals, and sensing His powers. His Church is the means to gain full access to all the blessings of God in time and eternity. To draw close to God's Church is to obtain a living and vital assurance of promises that are magnificent in scope and scale. While our love for others may endure eternally, it is only through Christ's Church that we can inherit eternal lives with our families. To give of ourselves to God's Church is to give ourselves to Him.

Make Our Word Our Covenant Bond

There are certain words, ideas, and concepts associated with God that apply to His covenants:

- *Promise, surely, shall, will, firm, steadfast* (see Helaman 15:10–17). God is intent on fulfilling His word. Such devotion is not incidental to Him. He does what He promises, swears, and asserts.

- *Remember* (see Moroni 2 and 3). The sacrament covenant is not one that God forgets. He remembers all His covenants. If God remembers something, that indicates it is of great importance.

It is important for us to know the sure, certain, and solid promises connected to God's covenants. As we likewise become secure in our performance of our obligations, we will find that our bond with God becomes unbreakable, ironclad, and resolute.

Enjoy the Protection of Covenants Faithfully Kept

Unfortunately, this message of covenant religion can often be ignored, misjudged, misunderstood, rejected, forgotten, treated casually, attacked, and trivialized (see 1 Nephi 2:11–16). However, it is still true and powerful. Likewise, we as covenant disciples can be misunderstood, persecuted, opposed, and so on, but we can still be loyal, true, faithful, and blessed. Easily made covenants tend to be easily neglected, forgotten, and abandoned when trials come. Procrastination is our enemy, as is trivializing that which is sacred. Fear and laziness are obvious obstacles to making and keeping covenants. Casual commitment needs to be replaced with quick determination that lasts a lifetime.

We need to value our covenants as being more important than worldly things. They are to be all-encompassing and embracing, impacting all areas of our lives. We are safe and wise to stay inside covenantal bounds. Their value is far beyond price. Honor, truth, and integrity are their watchword. They are priceless beyond material treasure. The covenantal ministry gives life meaning and purpose. As we abide in our covenants, we find a rich, abundant life. It is by cherishing our covenants that we display our devotion to God and others. It is important that we are aware, conscientious, brave, and dedicated covenant makers and keepers. We need to reflect thoughtfully on the agreements we are entering into and the implications of doing so. This is no small or trivial thing. We need to wisely consider our obligations, promises, duties, and responsibilities.

We need protection from being derailed, diverted, and distracted from the covenant path. Covenants safeguard us against our enemies and our own potential for error. We need protection not only from overt enemies of truth but also from more subtle attacks and arguments against faith and righteousness. We need safeguards against our own weaknesses and unaided wisdom. Covenants provide the precious protection we seek and need from both seen and unseen dangers. This is especially true when our covenants are entered into deliberately, honestly, and with introspection. Covenants that are valued and understood as sacred promises tend to be kept with more exactness, loyalty, and longevity.

Use Our Covenants to Bless Others

Our spiritual priority is to remain true to the covenant ourselves, help our families to be true to the covenant, help our fellow members to be faithful to the covenant, and help our friends to come to the covenant (see Enos 1:3–4, 9–17). When we comprehend that obedience or disobedience impacts not only ourselves but also our families, friends, and generations yet unborn, we are much more likely to cling tenaciously to our covenants and regard them highly. We sense that we live righteously not just to bless ourselves but also to benefit others. Our covenants extend both backward to our ancestors and forward to our descendants.

Help Gather Scattered Israel Home to Covenants

The marvelous work and wonder of the latter days is the gathering of Israel to the covenants of the Lord and the true knowledge of Christ. This is the cause of all causes, the greatest work we could ever be involved in throughout mortality. The blessings of the restored gospel are both personal and relational. They heal, bless, and save individuals and families. Jesus is the Lord of the gathering. He knows that the world is broken into factions. Both individuals and families have often been rent asunder through iniquity and conflict. As the scattering of covenant Israel came because of wickedness and unbelief, so the gathering of family Israel comes through faith and righteousness.

Christ seeks to bring individuals to unity with Him, to unite families together, to forge nations as one, to combine the world into one great body. Whether in the mortal world or the spirit world, He seeks to bring back that which is lost, to rescue that which is estranged, to redeem that which is wandering. We can feel confident that God has put forth His arm in these latter days to invite all to come to His saving covenant on both sides of the veil. His promises are eternally sure. There is hope and encouragement in spending our energies in bringing souls to the covenants of Christ.

3

Render Holy Gifts

There are many spiritual gifts God bestows upon us, and we can use these gifts to serve Him and bless others. Given their precious and impressive nature, the rendering of these gifts back to God represents a substantial offering.

Gifts can be desired for our own benefit. We want something and hope that someone will give it to us. Often these gifts are material objects. Sometimes they are opportunities to go places or to experience certain types of encounters. As a young boy, one of the gifts I received was a Chopper brand push bicycle. It had long handlebars at the front and inverted "U" bars at the back. I loved it. I cycled it to school every day. I felt cool, stylish, and important. Although it wasn't new, I regarded it as something that made me feel distinctive and powerful. I am still sentimental about that gift. It was far more than a means of transport—it was a token of identification. I felt like I belonged to a special club that only people with these types of bikes were allowed to join.

As we grow in emotional and spiritual maturity, we tend to appreciate gifts that celebrate our relationships, memories, and connections. We value presents from a deeper perspective. Over time, we can come to see gifts from our Father in Heaven in a new and improved light. We acquire a better understanding of what these opportunities mean to us and to those around us. For example, one of the gifts I have received in my life is that of knowing that Jesus Christ is the chosen Messiah of all humanity. This has made it quite easy to love, admire, and respect my Lord. I have been richly blessed to receive this knowledge. It has allowed me to weather many a storm and will no doubt continue to do so. This knowledge came in sometimes quiet ways. At other times, it came in dramatic ways. It has become very clear and powerful to me. It has been accompanied by peace, encouragement, and a sense of responsibility. This gift is not intended to be hoarded but instead to be shared with others. There is no gift I value more highly. I feel honored to have been given such a treasure.

Consider the following questions:

- What are some special gifts you have received in your life?
- What are the most important gifts you have given to others?
- How have these gifts endeared you to the people that gave them to you or the people you gave them to?
- What sentimental, emotional, intellectual, physical, social, or spiritual value did they have in your life or the lives of others?

You likely can recall at least some of these gifts and why they made such a difference to you and your loved ones.

The revelations of the Restoration are replete with the witness that spiritual gifts attend the Saints of God. These gifts are not without significance. They are powerful. They impact the souls of men and women. These gifts bless both the receiver and the other persons touched by the exercise of that gift. Thus, these gifts are often relational in nature. They make it possible for God to work through mortals to benefit the lives of other mortals. These important gifts are sacred. They bind us to others in loving concern.

I believe the best gifts are those that mean something to the person they are given to. They evidence that we are aware of them, we are thinking about them, and we love and appreciate them. We give them something to signify their importance to us. The fact that God gives us beautiful gifts evidences His trust and confidence in us. Likewise, as we mature spiritually, we will learn to give gifts to Him that matter to Him. He gives us His greatest gifts, and we give Him our best offerings in return.

While some days present us with material gifts like money, others offer us social gifts such as friendship. Some days involve intellectual gifts like listening to a profound thinker speak about a fascinating subject. Other days focus on emotional gifts such as being able to express our feelings about an important event in our lives that gives us some meaningful closure and resolution over happenings we perhaps had not explored before. All these gifts may be wonderful. However, I have come to sense that some days are especially important to us because they focus our minds and hearts on the things of God—the deep spiritual things that give essential purpose to our lives. In this respect, there are special days on which we give and receive holy gifts.

Holy Day Gifts

I love that the most special holidays were originally intended as holy days:

- Christmas celebrates the birth of the Son of God. The recounting of the Nativity reminds us that God gave His greatest treasure by sending His Son to save and redeem the world.
- New Year's Day was originally to remember the naming and circumcision of the baby Jesus. It encourages the forgiveness of others and to commit to beginning new and better habits in our own lives. What a gift to begin again and offer that hope to another. Which of us does not rely on new days, new starts, and fresh opportunities to be better?
- Easter commemorates the Atonement and Resurrection of the Son of God. It is only through the acceptance of the mission and mercy of Christ that any of us can lay hold on forgiveness. Immortality cannot be accessed by any other means. Such gifts far transcend the realities of sin and death in our temporary world.

All these days are traditionally family-focused and are intended to outweigh any work or other obligations. They are strongly associated with the giving and receiving of gifts, which points us to God-given gifts. We can rest from worldly sorrows and cares. These holy days give us opportunities to draw closer to God and others. True gift-giving can open hearts and minds to God's most precious gifts.

Needful Gifts

God has given mighty gifts when such were needful:

- King Solomon received great wisdom to judge matters in ways that would please God and benefit the people.
- The brother of Jared had the gift to get answers from God that would benefit the entire Jaredite family when they left the confusion of Babel to go to their promised land.
- Nephi was given knowledge of how to obtain the plates of brass through unusual means, strength to protect his people, and knowledge to build boats for his people to travel to the promised land in.

It is instructive to note that none of these gifts were given merely to showcase the greatness of these leaders but rather so that they might serve their people effectively. Gifts of God are given to bless! The gifts of heaven are to be distributed among the children of God in a way that there is sharing of each and all gifts. We are made spiritually free when our resources benefit our families, friends, and neighbors: "And they had all things common among them; therefore there were not rich and poor, bond and free, but they were all made free, and partakers of the heavenly gift" (4 Nephi 1:3).

Real Intent in Gift-Giving

God is concerned with our inner desires in giving gifts to Him and others. Only if we give with real intent—out of a sincere desire to do what is right and good—will we be acting in accordance with the design of heaven. Divine benefit only comes when our gift-giving is righteous. To give stubbornly, with resistance, is akin to not giving at all. There are no heavenly blessings for giving in this way. This is vital to remember when we offer our gifts. As it states in the Book of Mormon:

> For behold, God hath said a man being evil cannot do that which is good; for if he offereth a gift, or prayeth unto God, except he shall do it *with real intent* it profiteth him nothing.
> For behold, it is not counted unto him for righteousness.
> For behold, if a man being evil giveth a gift, he doeth it grudgingly; wherefore it is counted unto him the same as if he had retained the gift; wherefore he is counted evil before God. (Moroni 7:6–8; emphasis added)

Obtain the Spiritual Gifts of Christ to Bless Others

The gifts of Christ come to us through the Holy Ghost, which God has given to bless His children. We are privileged to receive these gifts so that we might honor God and help others draw near to Him. Indeed, such gifts help us to know Him in precious ways that would be impossible otherwise.

Consider the following truths about spiritual gifts:

- All spiritual gifts come by Christ's Spirit, meaning by His authority and sanction.
- They come in the form of one gift or many gifts as approved by the Lord (see Moroni 10:17).
- All persons do not receive all gifts. There are numerous gifts, and every person receives a gift from God through the Holy Ghost (see Doctrine and Covenants 46:11).
- The gifts are given to different people so that everyone benefits from all the gifts (see Doctrine and Covenants 46:12).
- None of these gifts would be ours without the Lord's express permission (see Moroni 10:18). He therefore has the right to direct their use and limit their expression.
- These gifts are only to be used for good purposes. They are gifts of goodness, as Christ is good.

These gifts are dependent on the faith of persons receiving them. We must have faith in Christ to exercise them. These gifts are everlasting, as Christ is eternal (see Moroni 10:19). The gifts require faith, hope, and charity, just as salvation requires these attributes (see Moroni 10:20–21).

God tells us that wickedness leads to despair, which obviously destroys hope. Conversely, righteousness leads to expectation, which aids hope (see Moroni 10:22). Faith in Christ allows for all essential things to be accomplished (see Moroni 10:23). Hence, the gifts of God cease among people who stop believing in Christ (see Moroni 10:24). This means their spiritual power ceases too!

To do good is to work by the gift and power of God. Otherwise, men are under wo (see Moroni 10:25). To stop believing in Christ—and hence lose His gifts and power—is to live and die in sin. Such persons forfeit salvation unless they repent before that dreadful day comes upon them. This is Christ's true word to His people through His prophets (see Moroni 10:26–28). God reveals the truth of His spoken and written words in due course to those who deny Him (see Moroni 10:29). To come to Christ is to lay a firm hold on *all* good gifts. It is to simultaneously avoid the evil gift and unclean thing—polluted counterfeits of the genuine gifts of Christ (see Moroni 10:30).

Now let's take a look at some of the gifts God blesses us with.

Knowledge Gifts

The gift of the Holy Ghost is given to us that we might know Christ now and eternally (see Moroni 10:7). Some are given the gift of knowing by the power of the Holy Ghost that Jesus Christ is God's Only Begotten Son in the flesh and that He suffered and died on the cross for the world's sins (see Doctrine and Covenants 46:13). It is very important that some in the Lord's Church have this direct witness by revelation. Some are enabled to know things and share that knowledge with others for the purpose of helping others to both know truth and live it in sensible ways (see Doctrine and Covenants 46:18).

Believing Gifts

Some are given the gift to believe on the words of those who know so that they might obtain eternal salvation based on faithfulness (see Doctrine and Covenants 46:14). It is important that some in the Church have this gift. Hence, in God's Church there will always be both knowers and believers. Both gifts are of God.

Discernment Gifts

The gift and power of the Holy Ghost is given to us that we might discern truth from error, especially with respect to spiritual things (see Moroni 10:5–6). Such truths will always lead us to accept Jesus Christ. God has given many spiritual gifts that operate in different ways. These gifts always profit individuals who accept them for what they are (see Moroni 10:8). To prevent spiritual deception, we need to seek the best gifts of God with sincerity and keep in mind why the gifts are needed (see Doctrine and Covenants 46:8). Some are given the gift to know which operations are from God and which are from another source (see Doctrine and Covenants 46:16). The manifestation of God's spirit is intended to be a blessing and upliftment to people. Some can discern spirits (see Doctrine and Covenants 46:23). This relates to recognizing whether spirits are good or evil, trustworthy or nefarious. This is a critically important gift to have when situations of potential misleading and deception arise. We have a generous God we can supplicate for help. The Holy Ghost will witness to us what we need to do with pure hearts and genuine obedience. Pleading and gratitude accompany our desire and focus on salvation. We are wise to know that we need to avoid the seduction of devilish doctrines or man-made commands (see Doctrine and Covenants 46:7).

A special gift of discernment is given to presiding officers to enable them to distinguish genuine manifestation of spiritual gifts from counterfeits (see Doctrine and Covenants 46:27). This is a safeguard to prevent or counteract the misleading efforts of those messengers claiming to be from God who are not in fact from God. The sheep of God could be led astray by dangerous wolves in sheep's clothing were it not for this special gift of discernment. Those receiving this gift are duly appointed and ordained. That is, they are called by the appropriate leaders through divine revelation. They are sustained in the accepted manner by the body they will lead. They are ordained to priesthood offices or set apart to callings, which gives them the authority to be shepherds, overseers, and watchers over the flock of God. Obviously, bishops, stake presidents, mission presidents, temple presidents, Seventies, Apostles, and Prophets need to have this gift, as do other leaders who may need to use discernment in determining whether their flock members are manifesting the gifts of the Spirit or some other power.

Wisdom Gifts

Some are given the word of wisdom (see Doctrine and Covenants 46:17). I understand this to mean the gift of wisdom, indicating the capacity to be wise and to teach such wisdom to others. Wisdom is the ability to apply truth in spiritually intelligent ways.

Teaching Gifts

The gift of teaching others to be wise is a spiritual endowment (see Moroni 10:9). The gift of teaching others to have knowledge is a spiritual talent (see Moroni 10:10).

Faith, Healing, and Miracle Gifts

The gift of having exceedingly great faith is a precious one (see Moroni 10:11). Such faith is accompanied by power to act and to achieve godly things. Some are endowed with the gift to have faith to heal (see Doctrine and Covenants 46:20). This clearly applies to those blessed to administer to others. Some are blessed with the gift of faith to be healed (see Doctrine and Covenants 46:19). This clearly applies to the person who needs healing from physical and other types of hurt. The Spirit of God endows some with the plural gifts of healing both oneself and others (see Moroni 10:11). Some are given the gift to work mighty miracles that are clear evidence of the power of God (see Moroni 10:12; Doctrine and Covenants 46:21). Obvious examples are Joseph Smith and Moses.

PROPHETIC GIFTS

Some are empowered to prophesy (see Doctrine and Covenants 46:22). This is concerned with directing the attention of others to fulfill the will of Christ through future acts. Some are given capacity to prophesy about *all* things. The future is opened to them in unique ways. More importantly, their testimony of Jesus Christ (being the spirit of prophecy) is a comprehensive witness of everything that our Lord has done for humanity (see Moroni 10:13).

VISIONARY GIFTS

Some people are given the ability to see angels and ministering spirits (see Moroni 10:14). I understand this to mean they can see unembodied, embodied, and disembodied spirits (see Doctrine and Covenants 129).

LANGUAGE GIFTS

Some persons are gifted to speak in tongues—and not just one tongue but sometimes more (see Moroni 10:15). Some can interpret languages and different kinds of tongues (see Moroni 10:16). This gift allows them to understand what others are saying. Some can speak with tongues and others can interpret tongues (see Doctrine and Covenants 46:24–25). The teaching of the restored gospel and the administration of a worldwide Church in situations where hundreds of different languages are spoken make this a very necessary and useful gift.

ADMINISTRATIVE GIFTS

Some have the spiritual gift to administer according to circumstances (see Doctrine and Covenants 46:15). This is a merciful reality because it means God suits His program according to the situation. The gifts of the Spirit are given to the people of the Church for their benefit and education. We are to be instructed in the ways and workings of God (see Doctrine and Covenants 46:1). The Holy Spirit directs and guides the conducting of all Church meetings by the elders of Israel (see Doctrine and Covenants 46:2). The spirit of revelation is needed for us to be about our Father's work! Bringing souls to Christ is a God-inspired labor. Hence, it is a form of spiritual gift to lead meetings in a manner pleasing to God and which will lead souls to God.

Leadership Gifts

Some persons are given access to all spiritual gifts because they are leaders in the Church and will ensure that the gifts so received will bless every person in their flock (see Doctrine and Covenants 46:29). This is most obvious in terms of the President of the Church, who holds all the keys of God's kingdom on the earth. He can use each gift depending on need and can discern the use of all gifts. His presiding leadership keeps order in the kingdom of God. All others are subject to his overarching righteous authority.

Cautions Regarding Spiritual Gifts

All these spiritual gifts originate with God and are intended to bless His children (see Doctrine and Covenants 46:26). The gifts bless those who love God and do His will and those who want to do His will. God is willing to bless all who come seeking such gifts if they have righteous motives in so desiring (see Doctrine and Covenants 46:9).

We are instructed to remember and to keep a focus on the spiritual gifts given to the Church (see Doctrine and Covenants 46:10). The gifts are not about personal aggrandizement, glory-seeking, or individual ambition. They are given to make a positive difference in our lives. Ultimately, they are given so that we might see our dependence on God and move toward Him.

Great opportunities for growth, companionship, support, and peace come through these gifts. Those who ask in Spirit receive in Spirit (see Doctrine and Covenants 46:28). Those in tune with the Spirit who ask for certain gifts will receive them. The underlying assumption is that those so asking are humbly pleading for the gifts in alignment with the will of God so that others might be blessed.

Chapter 3: Render Holy Gifts

The Lord is not obligated to give us any gifts unless we comply with His direction for how they are to be received and what they are to be used for. Spiritual asking must always be accompanied by using the name of Christ. Those things not done in His name have no divine sanction in time or eternity. We are to be thankful to God for spiritual blessings we receive. Our lives should consist of works of sacred purity always (see Doctrine and Covenants 46:30–33).

These are days of revelatory outpourings, sublime manifestations, and marvelous powers. The Prophet Joseph Smith righteously exercised all the spiritual gifts. Likewise, all who come to God with pure intent can sense these gifts when needed. Those gifts are given through faith in Jesus Christ, by means of the power of the Holy Ghost conferred upon us by legal administrators in the holy priesthood. These gifts build, bless, and benefit all the seeking children of God in time and eternity.

My testimony is that these gifts are real. They are expressions of the love and power of God. They are given to us in sacred ways that we may build and strengthen God's kingdom on earth. I have known many of these gifts in my life and ministry. I rejoice in these glorious gifts.

4

Rely on Christ's Power

Now let us explore some of the ways in which uniting with the Lord Jesus Christ can provide us access to His supernatural power. He gifts us power on certain conditions. As we use our agency for His cause, we can then do things in His service that make us and others better. Some things are simply not possible for us to do without divine help.

Power can be understood in various ways, such as:

- The ability to control people and events
- Strength
- An official or legal right to do something
- A natural skill or an ability to do something
- To act with great strength or in a forceful way
- Physical strength or force
- To provide something with the energy it needs to operate[2]

A light bulb is a wonderful invention. It may look lovely, cost much, and have great potential capacity. However, without electricity,

---

2. See *Cambridge Dictionary*, s.v. "power," accessed July 7, 2023, https://dictionary.cambridge.org/dictionary/english/power.

it will remain a dark shell of possibility. It serves no helpful function. It cannot provide light to a room. It cannot be a useful guide in a time of darkness. It has no power to be what it is supposed to be. Therefore, the light bulb really has no power—no purposeful usefulness—unless it is accompanied by the electric energy it needs to operate. In this sense, electricity is an essential power.

In similar ways, power is needed in all sorts of situations to make meaningful things happen. Physical strength is needed to chop wood, intellectual strength is needed to pass exams, emotional strength is needed to navigate tragedies, social strength is needed to weather relationship storms, and spiritual strength is needed to deal with mortal setbacks. We may need to rely on words to give a speech, use musical ability to play a violin, exercise discretion when we are listening to the confidential troubles of others, or showcase spatial awareness when we are playing sports. In these situations, we are applying some sort of aptitude, ability, capacity, or skill set we have learned over time.

The use of our hearts to feel, minds to think, bodies to act, and spirits to resolve allows us to develop capacities and fine-tune our abilities in significant tasks and a variety of circumstances. In this regard, we can develop a high degree of power to do things both for ourselves and others. Knowledge, skills, competencies, qualifications—all these things allow us to function in a demanding and multi-faceted way throughout our life. And power is not limited simply to skills we have. We may often find ourselves joining with others in causes that rely heavily on their unique abilities in addition to ours. Plus, we use the latent power of many objects in this world—such as levers, tools, and instruments—to allow us to do tasks that we could not do alone by relying on our own natural resources.

Sense the Power of the Lamb

Are there powers that the Lord Jesus Christ has that make Him uniquely qualified to empower us in every possible situation we face in mortality? The answer is yes. Let us consider some of His powers and what they mean for us in our lives and in terms of the service we can offer to Him.

Many times, I have admired the brilliant radiance of the sun in the sky. It has brought me noticeable warmth, light, and reassurance. These have been precious, golden moments, for even though they have been frequent, they are still magnificent each time. I love the beauty of the sun. It has blessed every person who has ever lived on this planet. It has helped every plant that has relied on it for the process of photosynthesis. It has made life on this earth possible. I believe that the sun in the sky is a symbol of the Son of God. He placed it there in the first instance. His power governs and controls it. But I am even more impressed by the power of Christ than I am by the sun in the sky because His power extends deeper and further than the power of the sun does. It extends into the eternities giving eternal life, while the physical sun is temporary and supports only mortal life.

It was only by faith in the Son of God that Lehi could receive the power of the Holy Ghost and thereby receive divine visions and the power to speak God's revelatory truths with convincing effect. Nephi relied on these same powers to learn sacred things himself. It was because Christ was the Only Begotten of the Father and the Messiah of the entire world that this faith in Him had such powerful ramifications for the peoples of the Book of Mormon and indeed people everywhere in all times (see 1 Nephi 10:17). The warmth, light, comfort, and hope that Christ gives is even more powerful than that offered by the sun.

It is by the power of Christ that the Book of Mormon has been preserved to come forth in our day (see 1 Nephi 13:35). This book gathers the sheep to the fold of God in a powerful way. It is by the power of the Son of God that other books of sacred scripture have and will come forth in the latter days to the convincing of the Gentile and Jew that the apostolic word concerning Jesus of Nazareth is true (see 1 Nephi 13:39). This includes books not yet revealed to the world, which can only come through the power of our Lord. The Savior has power to save the righteous. He can deliver them from the grave, sin, and the power of the evil one (see Alma 9:28). Mortals do not have such great power. Nor do heavenly bodies have such ability.

Appreciate the Beautiful Power of Redemption

Christ's beautiful power to rescue our souls goes far beyond the powers of transitory things. It touches every aspect of our being. I wrote a poem called "Being of Beauty" some years back that reflects my spiritual and emotional deliverance from the prideful antagonism of this natural fallen world:

>Falling downwards am I,
>I descend into darkness,
>Bitten by the snake.
>Wailing of the mourners is seen,
>My dejected heart
>Reposed in pity,
>Welcomed by the worms.
>These happy predators await eagerly
>The feeble foe.
>The sorrowful glance of onlookers who are distant
>Evidences their dreadful bemoaning of my fate.
>The poisoned chalice was fully drunk,
>The murky mists enshroud my mind,
>Thrown from the palace of glory,
>Cast down with wings of iron.
>Sculpted from lesser sod is my soul,
>Arraigned in princely robes I appear,
>But harnessing the power of defeat.
>
>Overcome by a deadly disease
>Toxic to both body and spirit,
>I wear the cloak of maggots
>Inside my body.
>Bereft of holy peace,
>I am the dragon's delight.
>The beast cheered me on.
>O wretched form,
>Misshapen and deformed,
>The inner man is as a mangled wreck,
>Adrift on a sea of sin,
>Cut through by the devils knife,
>Seductive selfishness slew me,

Self-broken through a thousand ugly deeds,
Split, fragmented, detached, serrated,
Fool of fools!
Is there any hope
For me?

I awake,
The dark terror of the night abolished.
O blessed day, this ray of righteousness,
O dear delight!
A chance has come before me
A second time,
Nay, a thousand times!
I will not retreat.
'Twas but a dreary dark dream,
This nightmare for men, like me,
Unless a transformation be wrought.
Lift the anchor, hoist the sails, set the course!
I am new forevermore,
O pleasant place with promise of peace.
Hold on, work on, hope on,
Cling tenaciously to the covenant of content,
Break down the lofty walls,
Dispense with the demonic dread.

Lift the glass of cheer,
Open the soul to gladness.
How can it be?
This is not my doing,
This is a better way,
This comes from a Mightier One—
A destroyer of darkness,
A bringer of tidings beyond comparison.
It is He!
The Being of Light,
This Man of Beauty,
This Friend of friends, Lord of lords, King of kings,
The Great I Am,
The Majestic Messiah.

> He has drenched me in His clean blood
> And I am rescued and restored
> To a palace of peace.

God has power far beyond that of humans. Further, He often invites us to do tasks that stretch us beyond our natural ability. In many cases, we are endowed with power from Him. This divine power—strength, force, ability, energy, authority—carries great might within it and allows for the performance of extraordinary things. For example, when the Prophet Lehi emerged through the mist of darkness to a place of love and light, he was teaching us a great truth (see 1 Nephi 8). When he partook of the fruit that filled his soul with joy, he was revealing a powerful verity. It is that God equips us with knowledge, perception, and power to see things, know things, feel things, and do things that we could not possibly do without Him. He empowers us with a new vantage point that gives us tremendous joy internally. He also strengthens us to be a source of help to those around us. The same principle applies to us as we navigate the world of difficulty and come to a place of peace. In the light of God's revealed truths, we gain added power to perform and accomplish all things that are expedient in the wisdom of God.

It is instructive to consider that we are not on earth simply to be good ourselves. We are also positioned to inspire others to do good. Further, we are empowered by God to be a source of strength to others. In this vein, it is helpful to consider in what ways God is willing to bless His servants so that they might both do good themselves and support others in doing good. In this sense, there are powers that God gives us that are personal to us. There are also powers that are relational in that they allow us to bolster others.

God gives strong answers to each of the following questions:

- What revelations could we seek for and obtain?
- What power to do good is in us?
- What decisions could we make, or what actions could we perform, that would please God?

- What promptings from the Holy Ghost could we follow to bless others?
- What gifts or talents could we use to build the kingdom of God?
- What service could we render to others?

We are promised that divine power is available to us. Indeed, if we have faith in Jesus Christ, "[we] shall have power to do *whatsoever thing* is expedient in [Him]" (Moroni 7:33). Whatever task our Lord requires us to do will be achievable with His help. If the errand He gives us is necessary, and we believe in Him, then capacity will be granted to us to perform our labors. We do not act alone.

Receive Power to Help Yourself

In this world of truth and error, it can be challenging when we are faced with competing ideas and values. This is why God blesses us with the *power to know truth* (see Moroni 10:4–5). We continually face temptations to do that which is wrong. However, God blesses us with *power to resist evil* (see 1 Nephi 22:26; Alma 48:17). We have capacity to oppose our tendency to yield to remorse-inducing actions.

We sometimes surrender to temptation. Therefore, God endows us with the *power to repent* (see 2 Nephi 10:25). This remedy is a glorious privilege and gift. Our lives are not without mistakes and failings. We have shortcomings, weaknesses, and flaws. We will all sense disappointment, regret, and error. However, these limitations are not the end of the story. As we come to sense our faults and sincerely rely on God, His help will become apparent in our lives. He will help us to fight the good fight, to overcome our problems, to rise above our challenges, and to put our temptations behind us. Ours can be a story of triumph and ultimate victory over the crude things of life. The empowerment that God gives us is one of resolute strength and determination. Each of us can embody the opposite of what now plagues us. Impatience can be replaced with patience. Fear can yield to courage. Doubt can give way to faith. Conquering the lesser things in life is something we can do well. The power to conquer weakness is a beautiful gift God gives us when we desire it and work at it.

We are often in situations where our spiritual values are decried and desecrated. We live in a time of a spiritual war of words, ideas, beliefs, and values. We need to be prepared to defend our cherished faith in God. Are we ready to go to battle? We need protection against false doctrines, addictive temptations, and enemy attacks. Our need is to properly ready ourselves by putting on the full personal armor of God. This consists of those principles and powers that come by divine appointment in revelation-based ways. As we strive to keep our spirits, minds, hearts, and bodies in tune with the revealed word of God—by hearkening to the messages of living prophets, the Holy Ghost, and the scriptures—then we will be ever ready to stand powerfully in the holy places of our lives. We therefore rejoice to be given the *power to be armed with righteousness* (see 1 Nephi 14:14; 22:26), *power over our enemies* (see 3 Nephi 28:39), and *power over evil spirits* (see Doctrine and Covenants 50:32). We can thus defend ourselves against onslaughts that will inevitably come from both the seen and unseen worlds.

We sometimes need visual instruction and memorable consolation. Hence, God bestows *power to dream dreams and see visions* (see 1 Nephi 10:17). We do not easily forget such experiences. We need more than human wisdom to guide us through the difficult moral and spiritual terrain we navigate nearly constantly in mortality. So God blesses us with *power to receive revelation from the Holy Spirit* (see 1 Nephi 10:17). The truth is communicated to us in a pure and intelligent way in this manner.

We are sometimes called to do difficult tasks for God. Consequently, He lets us have *power to do many mighty works in His name* (see Alma 19:4). Such great works are beyond human power alone, but we are glad participants thereof. For example, some men have been given *power to translate scripture* (see Doctrine and Covenants 1:29). I am grateful for this since I cannot read reformed Egyptian, Hebrew, Greek, or Latin! Even with great linguistic gifts, scholars cannot translate scripture without divine aid. This is primarily a spiritual work requiring more than great intellect. Indeed, there are many times when mortal gifts and talents are not sufficient. In these scenarios, God grants *power of endowment with heavenly gifts* (see Doctrine and Covenants 38:32, 38). Such bestowals bring about a heavenly work and a divine outcome.

This life throws many challenges at us. We are confronted in numerous ways with hurdles that test us. We would be defeated unless God granted us the *power to overcome all things* (see Doctrine and Covenants 50:35). In this way, no obstacle will ultimately overcome us if we call upon God for deliverance.

Music has the power to draw us close to God in majestic ways. Therefore, God gives us the *power of holy music* (see 1 Nephi 21:13). This involves inspired words and great music! It also incorporates both the singing and hearing of hymns. What beautiful power comes into our lives through righteous music!

In our world, we are not left without marvels—if we believe and trust in God. Hence, God grants us *power to do miracles, marvels, and wonders* (see 2 Nephi 18:18; Helaman 16:13; Doctrine and Covenants 45:8). Miracles may defy logical explanation, but they do happen and they bless many lives.

Our freedom to choose between good and evil is a gift. Our capacity to act for our welfare is so necessary in this world of testing. Therefore, God gives us the *power of agency* (see Doctrine and Covenants 58:28). To turn our righteous intention into action is a marvelous blessing from God.

The Church and kingdom of God cannot be run properly without divine aid. It requires a mighty arm to be effective. Thus, God gives us *power over Church offices* (see Doctrine and Covenants 107:8). His hand is manifest through His duly designated servants in a noticeable manner.

Although we are spirit children of God, we still need spiritual rebirth in this life. Hence, God gives us *power to become the sons and daughters of God* (see Doctrine and Covenants 11:30). This gives us added power and capacity to live the spiritual life. We believe that mortal life is but a prelude to a more glorious life beyond. Those eternal riches do not come automatically. Hence, God gives us *power to obtain all blessings, including immortality and eternal life* (see Doctrine and Covenants 138:51–52). In our union with God, we find the power to lay hold on all blessings.

Obtain Power to Help Others

God also gives us power to bless the lives of others as we progress through mortality. Consider the following.

Power to lay the foundation of God's Church (see Doctrine and Covenants 1:30). This power was given to Joseph Smith and other early Saints. While the foundation is already laid, we need to have power from God to continue to build on that strong foundation.

Power to baptize (see 3 Nephi 11:21–22). Brethren must be properly commissioned to baptize others. It is not a right we take unto ourselves. Think of it—we have power to give other mortals access to the kingdom of God on earth and the celestial kingdom in heaven. We also have power as living persons to extend these blessings to the dead. What a gift!

Power to bestow the Holy Ghost on others (see 3 Nephi 18:37). The power to grant others this great gift is tremendous. Think of the role of the gift of the Holy Ghost in your own life. We sometimes take His influence for granted. I have heard that those whose membership has been withdrawn lament the great loss of the companionship of the Spirit! One of the most important roles of the Holy Ghost is to reveal to us that without the Atonement of our Lord, no person could ever be saved (see Jacob 7:12). The Holy Ghost is a mighty preacher, a powerful testator, and a strong comforter. We need Him so that we can be all that we must become in these trying days of glorious opportunity. Even angels need to speak by the power of the Holy Ghost if their messages are to bring deep and lasting influence into the lives of mortals (see 2 Nephi 32:3).

Power to give the priesthood and callings to others (see Mosiah 25:19). Priesthood is the power to bless. Hence, to give the priesthood to others is to bless them to in turn bless others. Then those others will yet bless others. It's like a chain reaction or domino effect. We are blessing, guiding, and comforting God's children through the ripple impact of blessings. This would not be possible without the priesthood and the keys to direct its use. Think of the callings in the Church. Millions of people, serving for millions of hours, to bless millions of lives. This is a cause of rejoicing for God.

Power to minister to others (see 3 Nephi 7:17). To minister is to discern needs, to give voice to interest in people, and to notice the lives of others. It is to pray over, serve, watch over, and show love. To be effective in that labor, we need heaven's help. I am grateful that God empowers us to minister effectively to His children.

Power to influence others (see Doctrine and Covenants 121:41–46). Influence is not a small thing. Nor is it always a bad thing. We can be given divine power to influence others in love-induced, kind, caring, and benevolent ways. We can be a righteous example to others to guide them in heaven's ways. This is a positive help to them. It can impact them in meaningful ways.

Power over nations (see Doctrine and Covenants 77:11). The work of God is not to be impeded. It cannot be vanquished. Men and nations do not have the power to stop God from fulfilling His promises. If we need it, God gives us power to go onward, march forward, press upward. If we need power over armies, then we shall have it.

Power to seal on earth and in heaven (see Doctrine and Covenants 1:8). To bind the wound of a friend in this life is good. To save a marriage on earth is great. To rescue a family in this world is marvelous. Then surely to save and seal friends, marriages, and families in the eternities is glorious. To bring unity to that which is fractured is a godly work. I am profoundly grateful that God has blessed His Church with the power to unite for time and eternity all those who wish to be made one. Our ordinances and covenants have a beautiful power that transcends time, mortality, and the afflictions of a moment.

Power to seal up unto eternal life (see Doctrine and Covenants 68:12). Eternal life is that blessed state of existence where our ultimate hopes are fulfilled. It is the condition that incorporates a fullness of meaning and a full embodiment of joy. It is life to the maximum extent, life triumphant, life glorious. The fact that God would give us the sealing power as a people is an evidence that He is willing to grant us every good favor if we desire it.

Power to bring again Zion (see Doctrine and Covenants 113:8). Historically, the foundation of Zion has either been prevented for a season because of the wickedness of men, or having been established, it has been taken from the earth. However, this day and age is a time of spiritual destiny. We are to have a new Zion, a place of sublime goodness, a heaven on earth under our watch. We have power from God to build and strengthen Zion, and no force on earth or in hell can stop the Latter-day Saints from making this happen.

One of the greatest powers we have is to speak and preach God's word with great impact. This is a frequent promise throughout the scriptures (see 1 Nephi 2:14; Mosiah 13:6; Alma 17:3; Words of Mormon 1:17; Helaman 3:29; 6:5; Ether 12:25; Doctrine and Covenants 42:6; 138:26; Moses 7:13). We are to speak with the force of inspired words, revealed ideas, and eternal concepts. These mighty truths are to be accompanied by the Spirit of God. They are to be spoken, written, heard, and felt with convincing vitality. This is especially critical in our day when the voice of the adversary is loud and widespread.

Divine words provide the following special benefits:

- Teach critically important lessons
- Heal in times of difficulty, doubt, and despair
- Comfort with reassurance
- Warn about needed change, direction, or focus
- Protect from deception and tragedy
- Edify by bringing people to a higher, nobler sense
- Empower with courage to follow our convictions
- Miraculously impact in ways small and large
- Remind all that God's ways are sure and eternal

Choose to Tap Into Christ's Enabling Power

God can often persuade us to choose to change our own lives. Our beliefs, doctrines, and prayers give us power. We can exercise our agency in faith and thus determine our destiny through divine enabling power (see Doctrine and Covenants 58:26–28). This helps us to overcome feelings of powerlessness by taking charge of our own lives. We can alter our course when needed with divine help. Our agency can be honed as our desires are improved. In addition, we can sometimes influence others to divert away from danger and move on to glory. We can pay the price of deep discipleship over a lifetime. This brings the gift of God's trust into our lives. With such divine commendation comes more power to do and be good. As our humility is cultivated, so likewise is our faith developed, our hope renewed, and our charity fostered. As our courage is mustered, so can our knowledge increase and our diligence expand. Our lives can be touched, reformed, and redirected as we weather turbulent storms and scale mountains of challenge. In the acquisition of godliness, we find salvation. I know from my own experience that all of this is true. May God bless us with power to rise above sorrow, power to be who we are destined to be, and power to help the heartbroken souls around us.

5
Engage in Special Connections

The connections in our lives are of essential importance, especially the connection we have with the three members of the Godhead—our Eternal Father, our Savior, and the Holy Ghost. It is my conviction that by drawing close to God in relationship, we offer a valuable gift. Further, by choosing to have a living connection with these three special persons, we gravitate toward the true nature of perfection.

Connection is vital in our lives. God wants to connect with us. He also wants us to connect with others. There are many lovely words that suggest the need for us to be connected to God and with others: align, attach, belong, bind, bound, cling, commune, deal, depend, forge, fraternity, fellowship, friendship, join, know, link, lean, love, near, relate, rely, refer, seal, trust, unite, with, and weld.

We are socially relational beings. We live in communion with others. The connective tissue that binds us with others is deeply important. These associative inclinations come from our divine origin. We are interactive beings because God is an interactive being, whose good work "is to bring to pass the immortality and eternal life of man" (Moses 1:39). He is personally interested in us, our lives, our hopes, and our plans. As we benefit greatly from relations with others, so they benefit from a relationship with us. In like manner, we gain tremendous opportunity from connecting with God. He delights in His association with us.

God is perfect in His capacity to relate to us. He knows where we are coming from. He is aware of our limitations and our insights. He knows about our potential and capacity. He has a much stronger sense of our destiny than we do. He always has great capability to help us in needed ways, to direct us wisely, and to empower us strategically. His understanding of us goes far beyond what other mortals possess, even our parents, spouse, and close friends. His desire to connect with us is of great import. The significance of a relationship with the Supreme Being is of monumental importance to us. It is a privilege that ranks higher than any other.

It is vital to note that the relationship we have with God is not one-sided. It is reciprocal. It is mutually beneficial and reinforcing. It is a relationship of love. It gives something to us and asks something of us. It touches us in marvelous ways. It is satisfying, edifying, instructive, nourishing, and meaningful. To be impacted by God is to be moved. It is to be heard, to be seen, to be noticed, to be recognized. It is special because it is personal to us!

In addition, we are invited into connection not simply with one divine being but with three! We can each have a precious connection to our Father, to our Savior, and to the Holy Spirit. These three associations are enriching in a way that must be experienced to be truly understood. They are relations of enlightenment in that they give us a new way of experiencing the world.

It is also true that as we come to sense the connection we have with God, we come to discern that God wants to have association with each of His spirit children. We do not need to be threatened with any feeling of jealousy in these associations because we know that God is able to relate to each child in a rich and fulfilling way. He has power to form a strong bond of affection with each person individually. He caters to each need, sees each opportunity as important, and rejoices in each connection that is developed. This understanding helps us to act toward others in a way that is informed by divine understanding. When we see the divinity in others, we treat them in a more noble way. We want to help them to elevate their view to a higher way of seeing. We encourage them to connect to God, to seek Him out, to inquire after Him, to learn of Him, to love Him, and to continue in connection with Him.

Of course, our journey through mortality is an often scary one, a confusing one, a treacherous one, a lonely one, and a hard one. This truth confronts us head-on and starkly. It also brings us solace in that we come to expect and anticipate trouble once we realize that it is inevitable. Thus, we are enabled to develop a posture of strength in the face of adversity. Knowing that life will be hard prepares us so that we are not continually surprised and overwhelmed by this reality. Life is intended to be a learning ground. This means that there will be hardship. The difficulties we pass through are personalized to us in such a way that we know they are challenging. I believe that in our trouble we can call on God. We can rely on Him, look to Him, and come to know Him. He wants to share the moment with us. He is conscious of us, watching over us, loving us, sensing us, and rooting for us. He glories with us in triumph and weeps with us in trauma. The relationship He has with us is particularly significant when we travel through darkness and danger.

There have been many times in my life when I have been in an emotional and spiritual pit of despair. At those times, I have leaned heavily on my relationships with my Father in Heaven, Jesus Christ, and the Holy Ghost. I have needed the nourishing, nurturing, and sustenance provided by these important connections to bolster me. At one very dark time, I contemplated much on the significance of the love of God in my life. I felt strongly how incredibly essential the loving influence of these three divine beings was in my life. I literally felt that love—especially divine love—was keeping me alive and encouraging me to hold on. Heaven was my sanctuary, my refuge from the world, my solace in the floods of difficulty. My God was not a stranger then. He was aware. He was able to remind me, in quiet and gentle ways, that He was encouraging me onward. How important that recognition was to me. To feel that I was watched over and cared for was of deep import to my being able to weather the storms.

It is a gift to be in communion with God. It is a treasure to be in contact with beings who are without flaw or fault, who have no hidden agendas, who have no desire to hurt us. It is an honor to be able to feel known, seen, and loved by a mighty God, a true Father. It is helpful to feel that we have a Rescuer who helps us work through sorrow and sadness. It is a joy to have access to a Holy Ghost who guides us through every conceivable tragedy. Let us now consider each of these divine beings and reflect on how our relationships with Them represent both a gift They offer us and a gift we offer Them. These are not compelled relationships. They are voluntary—and that makes them so profoundly vital.

Get to Know the Holy Ghost

As we draw close to the Holy Ghost, He becomes our constant companion. Implicit in this is the idea that we become His constant companion too. We are associates in the work of the Lord. The notion of having a spirit be close to us might be scary for some people, as they tend to think of ghosts as dangerous or frightful, and spirits are often thought of as evil. However, the Holy Ghost is not an evil spirit. He is a righteous spirit. He is pure, loving, and holy. He is a commandment keeper, a loyal messenger from God. His role is one of guiding us in the path of life and light. To seek His company and yield to His counsel is right and good. I have found Him to be a true and trustworthy leader. To give heed to His promptings is a wise use of our ability to choose. To listen to His warning voice is to find a measure of peace—peace of conscience, peace of mind, and peace in our hearts.

Let us reflect on some of the distinctive roles of the Holy Ghost and how these functions are a source of great connection for us with the Spirit. The question might be asked, "How did you first get a testimony of God the Father and His Son Jesus Christ?" The answer for me is that the Holy Ghost delivered that message to me. He gave this precious knowledge to me. He lodged it in my soul. I therefore became connected to all members of the Godhead through the witnessing power of the Holy Ghost. We know that the prophetic word of God teaches us that receiving the powerful witness of the Holy Ghost about Jesus Christ as the Only Begotten Son of God is vital to salvation (see Helaman 5:12). That revelation-based knowledge will allow us to overcome every imaginable opposition arrayed against us. This is the sure foundation of saving faith in the mighty Messiah. In other words, we cannot build on the revelatory rock of our righteous Redeemer unless we receive this specific communication from the Holy Spirit. Connection with the Holy Ghost provides connection with all three members of the Godhead!

Draw Close to Our Savior

Jesus the Christ is known to us only to the level we seek Him—only to the extent we are willing to have contact with Him. He is revealed to us through serious reflection, thoughtful pondering, genuine study, heartfelt prayer, and receptive reading about His words, life, mission, ministry, and atoning sacrifice. Christ is known to us through the gentle yet encompassing power of the Holy Ghost. He is made known through the life and teachings of the Prophet Joseph Smith. Joseph is the clear and powerful witnessing revelator of the Savior in our day and age. This deep, abiding, and saving knowledge of the Son of God in our time comes through the revelations of the mortal seer who holds the keys of this dispensation—the prophet. Christ is known to us through the example of His prophetic servants, through the teachings and practices of His living Church, through the revelatory insights of sacred scripture, and through the doctrines, principles, laws, ordinances, and covenants of His holy house, the temple. He is known to us through His undiluted doctrine, pristine priesthood, stunning attributes, and marvelous Atonement.

Our Lord is known to us by walking in His way, through humble prayer, ongoing study, and consistent voluntary obedience to His loving commandments. He is known to us as we learn of Him, are changed by Him, find healing in Him, and strive for perfection in Him. As we receive instruction as His apprentices in His master ways, we become more and more inclined toward Him. Indeed, we become consumed in doing His will. The command to seek Him in close and tender ways is not a trivial directive nor a fruitless endeavor. It is an invitation with a promise: "Draw near unto me and I will draw near unto you; seek me diligently and ye shall find me; ask, and ye shall receive; knock, and it shall be opened unto you" (Doctrine and Covenants 88:63).

The promise of this scripture is clear. To move in the direction of the Lord is to have Him move in our direction. To genuinely look for Him is to locate Him. To request of Him is to find helpful response. To approach Him is to find His welcome. As we come to know Him, we become more resolute in abiding with Him always. We also wish to do our utmost to bring ourselves, our families, our friends, and even our enemies to Him so that they can find blessed association with Him. As we draw toward Him with full purpose of heart (see Omni 1:26), we find a new life, a better existence, a holier standard, a happier way. Indeed, we find a life of abundance. Others will also find a connection of tremendous joy as they find closeness with Him.

We truly have a Christ for all seasons of our lives (see Mormon 5:23). Whether we are thinking of holiday seasons (such as Easter and Christmas), seasons of rejoicing (such as births and weddings), or seasons of sorrow (such as funerals and heartbreak), we know that our Savior can connect with us in appropriate and beneficial ways. At these special times in our lives, and indeed always, we are seeking something. In fact, we are consistently searching for things in our lives. The most important quest we can be on is the one that leads us to the Light of the World, the Shepherd of our souls, the hope of our salvation. It is Christ we need to seek, as the Prophet Joseph Smith has pleaded with us to do. Whether seeking comfort in times of sorrow, a friend in times of gladness, an encourager in times of new hope, or reassurance in times of challenge, we can come to know that our Lord is the perfect associate for all seasons. Truly, inspired men and women still look to find Him. We seek Him with the belief that He will be there for us. We hope He will sustain us and rejoice with us. If we love Christ, we desire to share our lives with Him in such a way that we are both edified as we journey together. Our Lord is well suited to all seasons. He is both tough and tender. He is:

- Strong, Mighty, Powerful, Able, Reliable, Pure, Devoted, Determined (see Mosiah 16:9; Alma 7:13–14; 3 Nephi 24:2–3)
- Loving, Affectionate, Compassionate, Merciful, Forgiving—lifting and ministering to us (see Alma 26:15–20; Mormon 5:11; 6:17; 3 Nephi 12:44; 17:5–7)

Let us consider some of the ways in which connection with Christ blesses us and those we point toward Him.

Connected to Love

The nature of divine love is revealed in the compassionate regard that the Son of God has for each one of us. Without His pure, undefiled love, there could have been no atoning sacrifice for the salvation of humanity. Indeed, His traits are the highest and best embodiment of what it means to be good, true, and holy. As we come closer to Christ, we become partakers of the divine nature. We thus come to emulate the kind of deep empathic compassion that the Son of God possesses. Connection paves the way for compassion! To lead others to Christ is to connect them to the finest love that exists.

Connected to Healing

The Only Begotten Son of God is the great healer of our souls. He who knows firsthand the difficulties of disease has the power to give us beauty for ashes. Whether He heals us physically, emotionally, or spiritually, His effect upon us is soothing, aiding, and sweet. Whether He heals us quickly or slowly, He does complete the task. His ultimate purpose is to educate us in the principles of patience, understanding, compassion, empathy, sympathy, love, and mercy—for both ourselves and others. He will eventually heal our bodies and spirits as we come to know Him as the source of our salvation. Hence, connection provides full and complete therapy for our souls. To point others to Christ is to connect them to healing!

Connected to Growth

The Son of God makes us more than we are now. Christ intends to magnify each person who is willing to be so magnified. Regardless of our background, upbringing, or starting station in life, our Lord has the capacity and plan to bless us with increased capacity, ability, knowledge, understanding, and character. He wants to "add" to whatever we possess in terms of goodness. If we allow Him to teach us, He will enlarge our souls, expand our love, deepen our humility, and magnify our joy. As we believe in Him and follow Him, He can and will help us become the best possible version of ourselves. Hence, connection with Him gives us His kind and type of life. To encourage others to come to Christ is to connect them to growth!

Connected to Overcoming

I am grateful that the Son of God triumphed over the three great temptations presented to Him in the wilderness of fasting. He used His spiritual resources to resist the temptations of the pressing appetites of the body. He relied on His knowledge of truth to reject the sophistries of illusion. He focused on His dedication to His Father and repulsed the ambition of worldly honor. By following His masterful example, we too can transcend all weakness (see Luke 4:1–14, with clarifications from the Joseph Smith Translation). Hence, connection with Him gives us power to resist the fleeting demands of the moment in favor of the timeless standards of lasting goodness. To invite others to Christ is to connect them to power to overcome all the self-indulgent enticements of this fallen world.

Connected to Abundance

There is a sweet kind of life that is only known to true followers of Christ. There are mysteries we cannot comprehend until we come to put on His nature, His viewpoints, His feelings, and His thoughts. The scriptures teach plainly that the image of Christ is to be deeply and permanently etched upon us. We are to be living witnesses who reflect His profound goodness, strong virtue, righteous courage, and spiritual beauty. There is a different kind of life that comes to us through following the Son of God. The newness of life He offers us is rich in depth, beautiful in tapestry, amazing in scope, and never-ending in longevity. This new kind and type of life is majestic in time and eternity. The abundance of life He offers must be experienced personally to be understood and appreciated. Thus, connection with Him gives us access to modes of being otherwise unknown. To teach others of Christ is to connect them with gifts and privileges that would remain outside their domain of discovery otherwise.

CONNECTED TO CONSECRATION

God has said, "Prepare ye the way of the Lord, make his paths straight" (Doctrine and Covenants 65:1). There is such a thing as the way of Christ, the path of redemption. Not every person wants to travel this path or travel it to the end of the path. As covenant disciples of Christ, we are blessed to align ourselves with His ways, conform ourselves to His laws, and bend ourselves to His will. As we do so, we will discover joys that are deep and lasting. Thus, to connect with Him is to know the total yielding to divine ways that brings about the complete freedom that God enjoys. Moving others toward Christ is to connect them with a liberty that is optimal.

CONNECTED TO RECONCILIATION

The atoning sacrifice of the Son of God is essential (see Alma 34:9). We are instructed on the crucial truth that every person would be in a lost and fallen state eternally were it not that Christ performed a great work of reconciliation in the Garden of Gethsemane and on the cross of Calvary. Each noble soul, each striving improver, each mortal hero—every one of these would be without hope in the absence of Christ's powerful redemptive suffering. I marvel at His goodness and triumph over sin, death, hell, and the devil. He is truly the hope, light, and life of our world. I trust in Him without reservation. I am eternally grateful for the true doctrine that there is no salvation of any kind or degree in the hereafter without the Savior.

Each child of God gets to choose—personally and fairly—whether her or she will accept His offer of salvation and to what degree.

Obviously, this does not mean we believe in salvation by grace alone since that would fundamentally breach the idea of personal agency, individual responsibility, and unique accountability. Mercifully, however, Christ offers full salvation and full blessings to each one of us. He provides for different degrees of glory because He knows we choose to obey to different degrees. The extent to which we choose to follow Him, keep His standards, and comply with His ordinances and covenants sets boundaries and limits to the type and kind of salvation we will eventually enjoy.

All are capable of full glory. The conditional promise of eternal life only becomes realized when our acceptance of His Atonement becomes complete, total, and unyielding. I am sure He has power to save each person who is willing to follow Him with devotion. Hence, to connect with Him is to find not only immortality and a degree of glory but also to gain a personal appreciation for those reconciling blessings He gives to us. To focus others on the goodly Christ is to connect them with eternal gratitude. However good we think our Lord is, He is better! However strong we think our Savior is, He is mightier!

I feel connected to the Son of God. I know that the Savior knows how I feel. I have also come to know partially how He feels. I know my thought processes, my memories, my reflections, and my emotions. I know how I feel about my life. Of course, because He has felt my feelings and seen from my perspective, I have a sense of how He feels. He has felt about me how I have felt about me—sorrowful, remorseful, sad, and so on. Also, my feelings of delight, happiness, excitement, peace, and consolation are feelings He has had. I feel that He knows me and others from this unique vantage point. Through all the rich communicative means He has provided, I have come to associate with Him and feel blessed by His greatness. As I have tried to point others to Him, I have been blessed to see how they have also come to live in blessed communion with Him.

Decide to Belong to Father in Heaven

Our creation in God's image is literal. We are in fact His actual children, His divine offspring, His precious sons and daughters. We possess intelligence that is eternal—it can never die. We possess attributes of divinity, markers of greatness, and signs of wonder. We were born into this world to continue our climb toward a potential which is beyond our present capacity to imagine. Every marvelous aspect of God's greatness lies within us in embryo. I sense the truth and power of these majestic concepts. Through the restored gospel of Christ, we can ascend to the glorious destiny that awaits us. Let us climb upward, move forward, and stretch onward—and become all we possibly can in time and eternity. Our Father beckons us to the loftiest high place!

Let us ponder some of those marvelous ways we are blessed as we become more connected to our Father in Heaven.

Connected to Confidence

We are known and loved by the Supreme Being. Think of it! He knows each of us perfectly. He knows our entire life, our deepest interests, our mightiest struggles, our most sublime victories. He relates to us as His children. Our sorrows are seen by Him, as are our rejoicings. He has provided a plan of love for us that caters to our ultimate well-being. As we become aware of this great truth, we come to know and love Him too. We develop an honest relationship where we know that He knows everything about us and still cares for us. Likewise, we come to have a deep regard for Him even though we are imperfect now. Our efforts to draw close to Him are very worthwhile. Our connection with Him gives us the greatest and most lasting confidence in our lives.

Connected to Communication

Let us ponder the great power of prayer. I love the recommendation of the resurrected Christ in 3 Nephi, in which He encourages His followers to ask of God, seek God, and knock on the door that leads to God. We must pray to conquer the enemy of all righteousness. This exhortation is a powerful one. We can overcome the enemy of our souls as we ask fervently for divine help. To transcend the temptations, dangers, and opposition of our times, it is expedient that we seek the assistance of the Supreme Being. We can indeed put our petitions to

God, covering all areas of our lives. Our Father has time for us. He is inclined to listen to what we are inclined to say. While we might see scarcity, insecurity, confusion, doubt, and disbelief all around us, we can abandon this myopic perspective and discern that God is the giver of all good gifts.

As we supplicate at the throne of heaven, we will find that God gives abundantly, repetitiously, generously, lovingly, and constantly. His doctrine is deep. His revelations are rich. His gifts are great, and His blessings are bounteous. We need to ask in faith, plead with sincerity, and act with determination. His responses to us will be far beyond expectation. Prayer offers us closer communion with God, our Father. Martin Harris was instructed to pray always and by so doing would receive blessings of deep and lasting worth, more than any earthly treasures could ever possibly consist of (see Doctrine and Covenants 19:38). This is a powerful reminder that God is the living and loving source of all true treasure. As we commune with Him, we find knowledge, understanding, insight, illumination, and power to live a life of great richness.

Connected to Revelation

The word of God is to be spoken, heard, felt, and known in the latter days. The prophet Nephi instructs us that God is an ever-revealing being who seeks to share His precious mysteries with us (see 1 Nephi 11). As we approach God with genuine supplication, He will open windows of knowledge, doors of understanding, and vistas of eternal truth to our view. He loves it when we seek His counsel. I believe and rejoice in a revealing God. He is not possessive of His knowledge and understanding. He desires to share His purposes, plans, and promises with us. He has revelatory riches to bestow upon us. These deeply pervasive truths impact our minds, hearts, spirits, and bodies. They concern time and eternity. They probe into the past, present, and future. He wants us to know about His nature in sublime clarity. I am grateful that He speaks to us so that we can gain comprehension of Him. He will yet reveal many wondrous things to us as we seek in sincerity.

Connected to Spirituality

I believe strongly in the spiritual law of attraction (see Doctrine and Covenants 88:40). We are taught that intelligence longs for more intelligence, that wisdom welcomes greater wisdom, that truth rejoices in enhanced truth, that virtue loves increased virtue, and that all other divine attributes seek not only to grow and develop but also enjoy the company of all other righteous characteristics. Hence, the goodness within us admires and is drawn to the beauty of holiness resident in others. Ultimately, this explains why we are drawn to God with deep love and respectful desire to be with Him always.

Connected to Peace

I am reminded often of the need to lift my sights beyond the painful conflict all around us to look heavenward. It is so helpful to let God be our guide in matters of deep importance to us—such as our faith, relationships, and journey through this mortal world. We offer Him a gift by allowing Him to be involved in our lives. I accept the divine reassurances given to Joseph Smith while in Liberty Jail (see Doctrine and Covenants 121). Joseph was given peace. This peace would console, encourage, renew, and orient him. While it did not remove his heavy burdens, it did give him great and sustaining comfort. This peace is likewise given to us in our refining fires of affliction. We can be given peace to uplift us. This is very often the message of the Master of ocean, earth, and skies when we are tossed about on the seas of suffering: be at peace. This is especially pertinent in the time we live in, when contention abounds and persons are disillusioned. God is the Father of peace to our souls. Peace, beauty, hope, comfort, confidence, trust—these are divine blessings to the weary traveler who looks to God for help in the raging storm.

Connected to Happiness

I have experienced how obedience to God's commandments fills us with hopeful happiness and bounteous blessings. I also think about how communities of obedient people dwell in Zion, which is a place of peace. How consoling to know that the joy of obedience extends throughout time and into the eternities. If we truly want happiness, we need to seek it where it can be found. Surely the happiest being in the universe can help us to find this contentment. He can help us to point others to the happiness found in our Father.

Connected to Light

I glory in the light of God. This precious light is special due to its remarkable qualities. I rejoice that God wants to enlighten our minds with knowledge. Nothing is more valuable to us in time and eternity than the beautiful illumination that comes to us when we stand, kneel, and dwell in the majesty of God's glorious light. It takes His light for us to see others in the best light.

Connected to Vision

Our God is a being of marvelous vision. He has a rich perspective of those things that can be. He desires that each of us "catches the vision" of what life could be. This visionary viewpoint is revelatory in nature. It is the vantage point of heaven. We can "see" our true nature and the great opportunities and powerful privileges that lie before us. We can see in divine ways how we can become all that God intends for us to become. Then life will take on new and improved meaning for us.

Connected to Glory

I love the invitation of the Lord for us to have an eye single to God's glory (see Doctrine and Covenants 88:67). As we purify our thoughts, desires, and motives to align with the divine will, our bodies become beacons of light. We are then in a place where we can be properly prepared to see God face to face. This is the deepest longing of the spiritual soul. The greatest revelation we can receive is that of the reality, nature, and character of God Himself. His great desire is to have a permanent covenant connection with each of His children. The scriptures teach us the way to find this!

CONNECTED TO HEAVENLY JOY

The revelations of the Restoration given to the Prophet Joseph Smith declare that heaven is eternal and that the complete acceptance of Christ as the Only Begotten Son of God in the flesh gives us access to heavenly salvation. Saints who abide in covenant connection to Christ will sing hymns of rejoicing in this life and hymns of eternal gratitude in heaven. Great will be our everlasting joy in the presence of the royal nobility of the heavenly kingdom.

It is right for us to give everlasting glory to God. I praise our Father in Heaven for:

- Giving us life as His spirit sons and daughters
- Teaching and training us in the ways of light and truth
- Loving us with a demonstrable, perfect, and abiding love
- Providing an opportunity for each of us to come to earth to obtain a mortal body, gain experience, develop wisdom, partake in family life, grow in vital ways, learn to love truth and beauty, serve in life-enhancing ways, find a newness of life again and again, prepare for eternal glory, and bring others to the fountain of all righteousness
- Preparing a spirit paradise—a place of spiritual rest for us after this difficult mortality
- Shaping a kingdom of glory for our eternal resting home with family and friends

6
Experience Great Loves

There is a love so deep and majestic that it fills the heart and soul to fullness. This love is so wondrous that it amazes even the kindest person. It is so beautiful that it transforms the darkest night to brightest day. It is so sublime that it lightens the most seemingly unbearable load. It is a love so rich that it turns ingratitude to thankfulness, frustration to rejoicing, sorrow to relief, and despair to joy. I speak of the love that engulfs our beings with light and warms the coldness of life in replenishing ways. This love is within our reach if we know where to find it. It dwells within the God of heaven. It abides within the heart of Jesus Christ. It is carried within the spirit of the Holy Ghost. They have power to fill us with this most glorious love.

We were made for love, born for compassion, destined for sympathy, and created for empathy. We have the capacity, with divine help, to become great receptacles for love. We can be vessels of charity, beings of concern, persons of tender regard. Let us discuss how we can learn to love God, ourselves, and others with this divine love. This is a possibility with a promise.

Bridle Passion with True Love

Sin is not good for our souls. Giving in persistently to carnal appetites diminishes genuine concern for God, self, and neighbor. Hedonism decreases the loving regard we have for God, ourselves, and others. Hence, the Lord warns us that in the last days (now), the love of men and women shall wax cold because of iniquity. Pride, lust, greed, and anger are destructive of true love. On the other hand, true love has the power to overcome our natural proclivity toward base sensuality. The love of God powerfully impacts us if we let it. It gives us the motivation to put off selfish inclinations and to acquire the godly attributes of humility, virtue, selflessness, and gentleness of heart. True love conquers iniquity, overcomes the world, and prepares us for everlasting joy in heaven.

Feel the Sublime Love of God

Our religion is one of love. It is one where God loves us and we love Him. It is one where God invites us to speak to Him, share with Him, spend time with Him, and draw close to Him. This vertical love can have a sublime impact in our lives if we allow it to. As we love God with sincere intent, regard Him highly, respect Him honestly, admire Him gratefully, and appreciate Him conscientiously, we will come to value His guidance in our lives. As we share our innermost thoughts and feelings with Him, we will feel that the process of perfection is well underway in our lives. Indeed, the love God has for us is the most blissful, uplifting, amazing, and transforming love we can ever experience.

We can learn how to love God more fully. His love inspires us to be faithful to Him. Loyalty to God is the great challenge and privilege of life. It is thus the great joy of life. This divine love unites us with Him in profound ways. I believe that our divine identity should override all other demands on our time, abilities, resources, and devotions. I want to give beautiful voice to the doctrine that we can find unifying identity in righteousness through the divine love that permeates us as we try to love God with the kind of allegiance that He gives to us. I love my Father in Heaven. I am grateful that He knows that I value Him with great admiration.

Be Filled with Christ's Pure Love

Love is a treasure of the soul. Our Father in Heaven so loved the world that He sent His Only Begotten Son to this fallen world to save us from being hostages of sin and the bonds of death. Christ so loved the world that He gave His life as a ransom so that we could have our sins remitted and that our physical death would yield to new physical life in the presence of God. This divine love—this perfect charity—can be bestowed upon us as individuals as we come unto Christ. Like Nephi of old, we can become filled with the eternal love of God (see 2 Nephi 4:21). This quality of godly love fills us so that there is no room left for iniquity of any form. How wonderful that we can become living vessels of God's supreme love!

Learn Love of Self

It is evident that God is concerned about how we treat ourselves. He wants us to take care of ourselves, to treat ourselves right, to view ourselves as lovable. Many of us find this difficult to do, given the circumstantial backgrounds we face where self-love can be absent from much of what we experience. Internally, there are good feelings that God wants us to have about ourselves. There are holy thoughts He wants us to consider about our own lives. There are some useful questions we can ask ourselves to measure the temperature of our self-love:

- Do we regard ourselves and our dreams and hopes as important?
- Do we speak the truth to ourselves?
- Do we offer comfort and consolation to ourselves in times of trouble?
- Do we encourage ourselves through kind, thoughtful words?
- Do we forgive ourselves?
- Do we include ourselves?
- Do we say to ourselves "I love you"?

Learn Love of Neighbor

Loving other people is a divine commandment. It is an invitation to enter blessed association and rich union. It is an opportunity to give to another what belongs to us. When Christ asked us to love our neighbors, I believe He was speaking out of His own sense of charitable love. He cared for others. He asks that we care for others. He served others. He asks that we serve others. He ministered to others, and He anticipates that we do likewise. This horizontal love gives us opportunities to show our love among real people daily. It expects something from us. It also blesses us with the privilege of touching another human life for good. Clearly, our religion does not tie us to God alone—it links us with other mortals. Our felt, spoken, written, and demonstrated love for others is no small contribution to their eternal welfare. Our merciful forgiveness toward them is good for them! Our encouragement expressed to them may work wonders in their souls.

Share the Redemptive Love of the Lord

Alma asked the people he loved the inspired question, "Have you felt to sing the song of redeeming love?" (Alma 5:31). In other words, have you felt to sing the Redeemer's song of love? Have you spoken and sung about the Savior's redemptive act? Have you felt His atoning love? Have you shared that experiential love with others? Have you personally felt the charity of Christ for others? This indicates to us that we can and indeed should learn to feel these rich loving feelings of wanting others to be blessed with salvation. Feelings migrate to actions. Our felt love for others turns to good works for others.

The revelations teach us that the souls of men are valuable to God. The scriptures speak of the children of men in terms of their importance to God and how we should seek for the divine capability and comprehension to bring others back to our Father in Heaven: "Behold, O Lord, *their souls are precious*, and many of them are our brethren; therefore, give unto us, O Lord, *power and wisdom* that we may bring these, our brethren, again unto thee" (Alma 31:35; emphasis added).

Not all the people referred to were brethren of Alma, but many of them were. Some of them he had likely never met before. He did not know them personally. However, he still regarded them as precious souls. That is the spirit of this great latter-day work. We value the souls of men and women highly, both those we are acquainted with and those we do not yet know. Our interest is to bring them to God that they might find rest, peace, and joy in Him. If they have wandered, we desire to bring them back to safety and solace in the arms of their God. This is an expression of the redemptive love of Christ that has come to actuate our very souls!

Give an Unexpected Gift of Love

President Thomas S. Monson once asked members to give him a birthday gift in the form of doing something good for someone else. I was struck by that simple and selfless invitation. This great prophet was thinking of others. He used his influence to encourage others to bless the lives of people around them. To him, that was a gift he desired. He wanted to use the well wishes that we had for him to benefit others! A profound lesson for good is incorporated in this wonderful example. What blessings might accrue to others if we redirected benefits we were due to receive onto them instead?

Be a Witness of the Love of Jesus Christ

Many years ago, I had a unique "home teaching" experience. I still recall it because it was out of the ordinary. A middle-aged lady, who was a member of the Church but had not been very active in some time, was assigned to my companion and me. This lady did not live in her own home. Her son had committed suicide several years earlier, and she had blamed herself. As she constantly ruminated on his death, her self-recrimination began to fester. Her despair and self-blame continued to occupy her thoughts to the point that she became immobilized to everyday living. She was admitted to a psychiatric institution. It was there that we went to visit here. We "chatted" with her for a time and then left.

It was not really a conversation—it was one-way dialogue. We essentially listened to her string together somewhat incomprehensible words. As far as I could tell, this woman had lost, at least temporarily, the ability to engage with the outside world. She was locked inside her own recurrent stream of remorse and self-loathing. She seemed to me to be living in a kind of mental torture chamber, a prison of sorts, a hell on earth. I did not condemn her or judge her harshly. I just observed what seemed to me to be strikingly obvious—that this poor soul was captured by a situation that she could not break free from, at least not by her own efforts alone.

Now, I am not a psychologist or psychiatrist. I have no doubt that the professionals were able to detect her medical condition far more accurately than I could. I was there as a representative of Christ and His restored Church. I was there on behalf of the bishop to show concern and interest. I felt we lacked the power to reach her and give her any comfort or consolation. If we had been able to tell her that whatever the circumstances, she should not blame herself—if we had been able to get through to her the message of hope that there was a way out of this cast-iron cell and she had believed us—that would have been very consoling to us. However, it appeared that the difficulty was too far advanced at that point for us to make any real inroads. All we could do is show that we were concerned, even if she could not feel or sense that. I felt tremendous sorrow for this woman. Indeed, I felt pity. I wondered about all the circumstances that led to this point and pondered if it could have been avoided. Perhaps so. But at that juncture, it was a very serious condition indeed.

I did not see any human way it could be changed. It would require a divine way. I had that sense and feeling that our Savior understood this woman's plight in a personal way. He did not stand as merely an observer or even an interested party. He had a loving concern for her. He had walked in her shoes. He had carried her sorrows. He had felt everything she was feeling. He understood from the point of view of personal experience. I believe with all my soul that in due time, He will lift that burden from her shoulders. He will grant her peace such as she has never known. In His time and way, He will remove the stumbling blocks of mortality such as mental illness, guilt we take upon ourselves for the actions of others, and indeed all those dark things associated with a fallen domain inhabited by the adversary and his minions (see 2 Nephi 2, 9).

I am still somewhat haunted by that experience. The walls were painted gray and really were quite depressing. I thought to myself, "If people are feeling bad when they come in here, this ambience will do nothing to improve their mood." It was a somber experience. I look forward to that day when the sorrows associated with such mortal tragedies are remedied. Christ is our great compensator. Looking to Him now gives us hope through the darkness of such traumatic life events as the loss of children to suicide and other terrible things in our lives. Even though it appeared we had no visible success in trying to communicate our hope in Christ for this lady's painful ordeal, I am still glad I went. I believe we sat with her in her pain. Christ sits with us in suffering. The situation may not be resolved immediately, but it will be made right in the due time of the Lord. One day, this lady will come to know that Christ is the remedy for all maladies—not just for her own sorrows but for her son's tragedies too.

In this regard, our love of others is manifest in trying to console, encourage, help, aid, and support them. Our love may not always appear useful or appreciated. However, it is a testament to our effort, desire, and intention. It is our witness of Christ in His role as Healer, Comforter, and Redeemer. Surely, our Lord rejoices when we share our gifts of love with others in such ways. We are made better by such encounters, and eventually others are likewise blessed.

Reach for a More Excellent Love

It breaks my heart to see the animosity, conflict, contention, hatred, contempt, and anger in our world. Interpersonal relationships and nations are made weaker when dissension abounds. I have often thought about how Christ offers us a "more excellent way" of His pure love. I believe His love changes the way we relate to every person we meet. His love abounds within us when we bridle all our passions. This excellent way is the strait and narrow path of obedience to divine commandments. As it says in Moroni 7:45, "Charity suffereth long, and is kind, and envieth not, and is not puffed up, *seeketh not her own*, is not easily provoked, thinketh no evil, and rejoiceth not in iniquity but rejoiceth in the truth, beareth all things, believeth all things, hopeth all things, endureth all things" (emphasis added).

Imagine what would happen if this pure Christlike love filled our world. We can scarcely envision such a world! I am convinced that Christ can heal the world—one person at a time. He can remove antagonism from our hearts and fill us with His own love. He can heal any who come to Him in humility. I look forward to that "soon-to-come" day when Christ will come to heal the entire world. Until that day comes, I want to walk in the way of the Prince of Peace. I have a firm hope in Him. I know that as we exemplify His divine love, we are contributing to the transformation of the world.

Nourish the Beautiful Legacy of a Life of Love

Love is an important thing to feel, experience, do, and share. Indeed, it is essential. Mortality without giving and receiving love is a form of spiritual poverty. We want to live well and love well. To love God, ourselves, and others is a rich encounter with things of transcendent worth. Our love is given to us to share. It is a gift we can give to our Lord and our fellow beings on the road of life. Far more important than the physical things we leave behind on departing this mortal life is the spiritual legacy of faith we leave. The highest form of love is tied to the true and living God. If we have been sincerely yoked through covenant to God and Christ, we can depart this life with the hope of a glorious resurrection (see Doctrine and Covenants 42:45). We can assure our loved ones who remain on the earth that we are at restful peace with the certain promise of life everlasting. That is the kind of wonderful legacy of love the God of heaven wants us to claim for ourselves and our loved ones.

7

USE PRECIOUS BELONGINGS

EACH OF US POSSESSES VALUABLE BELONGINGS, AND IT IS EVIDENT from the revelations of heaven that we are asked to give these special belongings to God if we desire to go where He is and do what He does. This includes offering our heart, might, mind, and strength to the great cause of Christ in mortality. Another way of saying this is to refer to devoting our feelings, spirits, ideas, and bodies to the highest and noblest cause. These refer to the entirety of our spiritual and temporal makeup—they include all that makes us a unique and distinctive person. As we choose to use these personal belongings in the service of God, we will be giving something truly precious to Him.

Early in this dispensation and before the Church was established, the Lord gave us some personal qualifications that we need to understand and develop if we are to give the innermost parts of ourselves to God. If we are to align our spirits, bodies, hearts, and minds in a righteous unity, we need to know God's very clear directions and requirements:

> Now behold, a marvelous work is about to come forth among the children of men.

> Therefore, O ye that embark in the service of God, see that ye serve him with all your *heart, might, mind and strength,* that ye may stand blameless before God at the last day.
>
> Therefore, if ye have *desires* to serve God ye are called to the work;
>
> For behold the field is white already to harvest; and lo, he that *thrusteth in his sickle with his might,* the same layeth up in store that he perisheth not, but bringeth salvation to his soul;
>
> And faith, hope, charity and love, with an eye single to the glory of God, qualify him for the work.
>
> Remember faith, virtue, knowledge, temperance, patience, brotherly kindness, godliness, charity, humility, diligence.
>
> Ask, and ye shall receive; knock, and it shall be opened unto you. Amen. (Doctrine and Covenants 4:1–7; emphasis added)

In this revelation, God tells the Prophet Joseph Smith that a marvelous work is about to happen among men. This clearly refers to the outpouring of gifts and powers that would attend the servants of the Lord in these remarkable, unusual days. We can be involved in God's unique miracle. This work is truly extraordinary, astonishing, surprising, and amazing.

We learn that those starting to serve God should ensure they have invested their heart, might, mind, and strength. Implicit in this invitation is the assurance that we *can* serve God with all our heart, might, mind, and strength! God does not give us impossible commandments. We can only stand without blame at the last day before God if we have learned to serve Him in a way that involves our whole soul. The order in which these attributes are placed in scripture suggests something significant. It is only when our hearts and minds are turned to God that our spirits will exert a significant influence over our bodies to perform the actions that are both necessary to, and evidential of, our faith. Let us consider the implications of each of these directives.

Heart

A dictionary definition of the word "heart" might be "the part that feels, loves, hates, and desires, the seat of one's inmost thoughts and secret feelings." Words that are figuratively associated with the heart might be love, affection, devotion, kindness, sympathy, compassion, spirit, courage, enthusiasm, determination, resolution, fortitude, disposition, temperament, or character.

For example, it was the profound *desires* in Joseph Smith's heart that he offered up to God in prayer before he received the visitation of God the Father and God the Son (see Joseph Smith—History 1:15). Such a deeply sincere request brought forth a genuine response!

Might

A dictionary may indicate that the word *might* reflects the use of all one's power and strength. There is an implication of the full range of one's ability being employed, with no reservation or holding back. God loves it when we give all to His work.

Mind

A dictionary might say that the mind involves the part of a person that knows, thinks, feels, wishes, and chooses. It indicates desire, purpose, intention, and will. A purposeful and intentional person can do wonders in the work God has for them.

Strength

A dictionary might refer to *strength* as consisting of power, force, vigor, toughness, capacity to endure, or the quality or condition of being strong. When speaking of the word *powerful*, the dictionary would suggest the meanings of having great power or force, mighty, strong, authority, right, control, or influence. A person who gives their strength to God has used their natural endowments for a worthwhile cause.

I believe we are given great strength or power in certain aspects of our lives so that we might do much good for God and those around us:

- Great physical strength—so we can perform hard work and protect others from threat. Our strength should be used to safeguard others who may need our physicality!

- Great intellectual strength—so we can have ideas to do good and support others. We are given such strength to assist others who need our intellect!
- Great emotional strength—so we can listen and help others. It is intended that we would support others!
- Great spiritual strength—so we can lead and guide others rightly. This is given so we might encourage others!

The scripture teaches that if we want to serve God, then He will call us to such service. *Desire* is a necessary prerequisite to please God. This revelation refers to laying up in store. What are we laying up in store by serving God with all our souls? We are laying up the treasure that belongs in heaven! We will receive such heavenly rewards *after* we treasure God on earth (see Matthew 6:20). Treasure means valuable things. To treasure something is to value it highly, cherish it, or prize it. If we value God and His children, we will cherish them on this earth! We will show them that they are more important to us than other concerns or demands. It is by putting God and His children highest on our list of mortal priorities that we lay up heavenly rewards. That treasure is eternal life, or God's greatest gift to His children. Hence, to gift ourselves to God now is to receive His ultimate and best gift in the celestial heaven that awaits us.

We are further informed that we need to be *qualified* for the work of God. To have the attributes of godliness is to be qualified for God's work. To qualify something is to make fit or competent, to prepare or equip. Thus, to be ready and able to do the Lord's work in the latter days requires that we acquire the personal attributes that belong to divinity, at least in a measure. We do not become capable servants of God without effort, intention, and sacrifice. We are to be shaped, molded, and trained. Indeed, we are asked to have an *eye single to the glory of God*. Hence, personal ambition is to be rooted out. Love of God, the praise of God—these are core to our service if we seek to give God all we have and are.

God mentions specific qualities that make us suited to His work. These personal attributes center around believing in Christ, trusting

Him, relying on Him, loving Him, caring about Him, seeking to be pure like Him, wanting to learn what He knows, having discipline like He does, waiting on the Lord, being kind, being a holy person, cultivating meekness, and being dedicated to our service. Finally, we are invited to ask God for help. He will give it to us! We are commanded to seek Him, and He will make Himself known to us.

If we consider this revelation in totality, it is apparent that God is looking for us to be invested in Him, be loyal to Him, and be close to Him. He wants us to regard Him and His ways highly. He wants us to use all our resources—whether spiritual, mental, emotional, or physical—to serve Him and His children. This is all we can possibly give to Him. It is to dedicate our spirits like His noble spirit is devoted. It is to fashion our bodies to His image and likeness. It is to think on Him, feel after Him, and live like Him. It is to concentrate our efforts on His cause. It is to love His children with a pure love. It is to safeguard against evil and promote goodness throughout the earth.

Offer a Gift in Trust

It is evident that God views the mortal body with great respect. Moral purity is one of those very special gifts God has asked us to safeguard with prudential regard. Let us therefore consider what applicability moral purity has in terms of offering a sacred gift to God. The question might be asked, "Why does God ask us to reserve intimate relations for the marriage covenant between a man and a woman?" Perhaps a thought experiment given in something of a parable form will assist in this vital issue.

Let us suppose that you kept a personal journal for many years. Let's imagine that this journal was not filled with trivial details of your life. Rather, it was replete with many of your special insights, genuine feelings, deep worries, anticipatory hopes, and innermost thoughts. That would be an especially important treasure to you. You would keep it safe. You would not throw it out or allow it to be lost. You would not share it with those you did not trust. You would not speak openly about the secrets contained in your journal. You would safeguard it by not sharing it with casual acquaintances or enemies.

This journal in many ways is analogous to your mortal body. Your body is a gift. It is not to be treated like garbage. It is not to be valued cheaply. It is not to be undermined, abused, or cast aside—either by you or others around you.

Our bodies are far more important than some things over which we have great concern, such as houses, cars, sentimental items, and jobs. These things are important in their time and season, but they can never be more important than the gift God has given us of being clothed with a tangible, mortal tabernacle. The sharing of our selves with others is to be carefully managed according to the plan of God—within the bounds of covenantal love. A sense of the sacred makes all the difference in the world to what we do with our lives. It is difficult to act in holy ways without at least a degree of holy understanding.

When someone comes into our lives who values, respects, and loves us, then we can consider becoming yoked to them through marriage—the spiritual union through covenant of a man and a woman in the plan of God. Such a marriage is founded on trust, faith in Christ, reverence for life, and respect for moral intimacy. In these exceptional circumstances, we can share our personal journals with a spouse who hopefully will treat our sacred treasures with due respect. Likewise, and more importantly, they will treat our bodily gift to them with gospel-based righteousness. There will be no room for abuse, misuse, or mistreatment.

Of course, relations within the bounds of spiritual matrimony highlights the holistic understanding that marriage partners share their minds, hearts, bodies, and spirits with each other. To offer the gift of ourselves to another in trust is the greatest act of trust we can ever take. It is not to be performed lightly. The gift is given in trust. It should also be received in trust. That which is sacred is to be valued with the utmost sensitivity. Otherwise, relationships are breached, damaged, and may be exceedingly difficult to repair. On the positive side, where such relations are respectful, they are also enriching and enable flourishing in both parties. I therefore believe that God invites union—whether spiritual, physical, emotional, or mental—on the strict basis that it be done according to His superior understanding of what works, what blesses, what saves, and what protects. He knows how to elevate us to where He is. This is also why I feel that it takes faith to resist moral temptation. It takes belief to marry right. It is only on the other side of taking that step of faith that we find the rewards. God wants us to come to know this holy offering on a human level.

In an analogous manner, God knows that by offering our heart, might, mind, and strength to Him in service, our natures can blossom fully. To trust God is not to make a mistake. We can share our lives in His cause without Him ever breaching our trust, manipulating us, tricking us, betraying us, abusing us, or denigrating us. Instead, His reception of our gift will be warm, responsive, appreciative, thankful, glad, generous, and reciprocal. He takes our secrets and safeguards them. He hears our wishes and promotes them. He knows our abilities and enlarges them. Our efforts to change for the better are ones He encourages. Our doubts are ones He acknowledges and replaces with assurance. Our anger is swallowed up by Him and turned to thankfulness. Our weakness is conformed to strength in Him. Our sadness gives way to rejoicing. Our hurt is blanketed by healing.

Let us take the example of Jared and his brother. They and their people were amid trouble when the language of the people at the Tower of Babel was confounded. We learn in the book of Ether that the Lord heard the prayers of these two brothers. When they prayed for their language not to be confounded, their prayer was heard. When they prayed for guidance, their petitions were received. When they prayed for a way to have light in their boats so they could travel to the land of promise, God supplied a way.

I have always loved that the stones became lighted by the touch of Christ. For me, the boat might be regarded as comparable to the mortal body, while the persons inside might be likened to our spirits. We trust our boats (bodies) on the rough waters of life (opposition and difficulty) only to those who have our true interests at heart—other family members who love us and especially our great and trustworthy God. Similarly, we might regard the boat as a symbol of the family, or of the Church, or of a holy tabernacle. It was—like the earlier ark of Noah, or the boat Nephi would later build—akin to a portable temple. The physical boats were symbolic of a covenant of love and belonging between Jehovah and His people. It required faith and trust to build, enter into, and stay in those boats. That trust would be rewarded by God's sure character.

I see great significance in this. Christ is the Light of the World (see Matthew 5:13–20). Hence, the stones of light were essentially stones of Christ, or symbols of the Lord. Christ is therefore the light of the boat! Think of that—Christ is metaphorically and symbolically in the boat with the Jaredites as they travel on the rough seas toward their new land of hope. President M. Russell Ballard has invited us to stay in the boat when troubles surround and confound us.[3] What he meant is that we should stay in the Church—or the family, or the temple—when the waves and winds are rocking the boat.

When I combine President Ballard's counsel with the message of Ether 3, I see that we are to stay in the boat of Christ. In other words, we stay in the family of Christ, the Church of Christ, the temple of Christ. We stay because the Savior is there with us. Just as our Lord calmed the seas when the disciples feared and awoke Him (see Mark 4:38), He is with us in the boat today! We do not need to jump overboard. We should not try to steer the ship ourselves or say the Lord does not care if we perish or not. He cares! He speaks! He leads! He controls the ship! He directs the family! He presides in the temple! We are wise when we trust our most precious gifts to those who are reverential toward such offerings.

Serve God in Love

"Thou shalt love the Lord thy God with all thy heart, with all thy might, mind, and strength; and in the name of Jesus Christ thou shalt serve him" (Doctrine and Covenants 59:5).

This verse is simply to promise that when we offer our bodies, spirits, hearts, and minds to God, He will bring us from realms of danger to the places of peace that our souls so earnestly desire. To trust Him is to honor Him and His word:

---

3. M. Russell Ballard, "Stay in the Boat and Hold On!," *Ensign* or *Liahona*, Nov. 2014, 89–92.

- We give Him our mind because He can direct our thoughts right.
- We give Him our heart because He can bless us with wonderful feelings of joy and peace.
- We give Him our body because He knows how to deliver the body from death and the grave.
- We give Him our spirit because He alone can save it from hell and the devil.

Similarly, as we encourage others to "seek this Jesus" (Ether 12:41), we are commending them to someone who will treat them in a way that will bring the greatest good to bear in their lives. We will bless them by inviting them to come unto Christ.

8
Display Significant Tokens

As we grow in the gospel of Jesus Christ, there are certain tokens we can offer to God that reflect our spiritual maturity. A token is an indicator of something. It is a marker of that which is precious. In the gospel sense, tokens are those things that exemplify Jesus Christ and His marvelous efforts on our behalf. For example, the wounds He received on the cross of crucifixion are regarded as sacred tokens displaying His love for humanity. He was pierced violently. Those six imprints—two in His hands, two in His wrists, one in His feet and one in His side—are evidence of His atoning sacrifice to save our souls. His love is shown in suffering that saves. As Christ displays His love through the manifestation of His tokens, we likewise can show our great love for Him and our brothers and sisters by means of tokens.

Our token offerings show the vital importance we place on Him and His life and ministry. By so doing, we evidence clearly that we are giving our greatest gifts to Him. Indeed, the Book of Mormon invites us to render to God "all that [we] have and are" (Mosiah 2:34) and to render to "every man according to that which is his due" (Mosiah 4:13). Modern revelation instructs us to "render unto Caesar the things which are Caesar's" (Doctrine and Covenants 63:26). Some token offerings that we can give to God include our time, talents, and treasures.

The Gift of Time

Today is the time of our salvation (see Alma 34). There is a sense of importance attached to this moment, this hour, this day, this week. This mortal time is more vital to us than we sometimes suppose. It lays the groundwork for that which comes in the next life. Therefore, the gospel discourages procrastination. This inspires us to obey now and decisively, to repent now and quickly, to act now and deliberately. Now is the wonderful time to prepare for eternity. We can know, at least to a certain extent, the great blessings that come from humbling ourselves with soft hearts without being continually compelled to do so. As we do so, God will pour out peace, promptings, and strength into our lives. We will rejoice exceedingly. We do not regret using our time to do good and be good. I personally do not regret any sincere righteous thing I have done. I do feel sorrow for bad things I have done and good things I have left undone.

I also believe that we can progress toward salvation more quickly if we choose to. We can actively choose to learn truth at a quickened pace. We can show enhanced observation to God's will and approach Him as truth seekers more fervently and frequently. I believe that one of the keys in finding God in this life is to intentionally push ourselves to do far more than the minimum. In the examples of prophets and Saints of all ages, we find that those who sought the Lord early found Him sooner than they otherwise would have. If we decide to offer our gifts to God and our brothers and sisters, then God will give us those opportunities in special ways. If we do this soon, He will respond soon. This is a great and powerful secret that can come to inform our discipleship in marked ways.

Last year, I was pondering on the forty-day fast of the Savior in the wilderness: "And after forty days, the devil came to him, to tempt him. And in those days he did eat nothing: and when they were ended, he afterward hungered" (Joseph Smith Translation, Luke 4:2 [in Luke 4:2, footnote *a*]). Moses also fasted for forty days in a high mount setting (see Deuteronomy 9:9). Both experiences were entered into in a spirit of desire to receive divine instructions and to obtain fortification for the days ahead. As we know, Christ began His three-year ministry after His experiences in the wilderness. Moses received the Ten Commandments, which would guide the people of Israel during his time and would come to shape the destiny of the Judeo-Christian world for centuries to come.

While pondering these scriptural realities, I determined that a forty-day period of spiritual experience would be useful in my life. Instead of physically fasting for forty days, I decided I would listen to every conference talk of President Russell M. Nelson over a forty-day period in preparation for the April 2022 general conference. Since he had given nearly a hundred talks since April 1984 when he was sustained as a member of the Quorum of the Twelve, I knew I would need to listen to two to three talks per day to accomplish the task. That required me to dedicate time to this task when I could focus and not be interrupted. I would spend around thirty minutes per day fulfilling this personal promise. I would need to sacrifice and consecrate this time to the Lord as an indication that I wanted to "hear Him" and "let God prevail" in my life more fully. I have found the experience highly beneficial. Here are some lessons I have learned or been reminded of.

President Nelson has been teaching over the last forty years some of the core doctrines and principles he teaches now. I have discovered that if we want to know what a prophet will be teaching twenty or thirty years from now, we can listen to each of the Apostles now to see what they are focusing on. This will give us advance indication of what is yet to come. The teachings of an Apostle will often surface again upon their becoming the living prophet, so it is important to listen to each Apostle now—even the most newly called! The Lord is thus trying to reach us both now and into the future by this carefully constructed means of preparing His people. There is an insulative and protective power that comes to us from hearing and heeding the words of our prophets.

The messages of prophets are rarely, if ever, in line with current cultural fads and fashions. They do not seek to declare that which is popular or worldly but rather that which is true. Prophets primarily are special witnesses of the name of Christ in all the world. They teach His doctrine, perform His ordinances, invite people to come to His covenants, and build up His kingdom. In this they are often hated, maligned, criticized, and ignored. However, they are also loved, admired, appreciated, and followed. Their primary concern is with those things that strengthen the Church and kingdom of God. I believe they are willing to give their lives in sustaining and defending the restored gospel of Christ as revealed to Joseph Smith. So the appropriate test of a prophet is not whether we like what they are preaching but whether it aligns with the designs of God. Their message will, in the words of President Harold B. Lee, "comfort the afflicted and afflict the comfortable."[4]

I discerned many core truths that President Nelson has always exemplified in His apostolic ministry:

- The law of God is compatible with His love.
- Heeding the counsel of living prophets will always benefit and bless us.
- Covenants made and kept are an anchor and safety to the soul.
- Faith in Jesus Christ is powerful, motivating, and triumphant.
- Family life as designed by the Lord is the foundation and springboard for true spirituality and joy.
- The work of salvation is core to the Church and to our lives as covenant Israel. Our responsibility is both a burden and a privilege.
- Revelation is ongoing and needs to be actively pursued.
- The Second Coming of Christ is worth preparing for now.

---

4. See Harold B. Lee, *New Era*, Jan. 1971, https://site.churchofjesuschrist.org/study/new-era/1971/01/the-message-my-dear-young-fellow-workers?lang=eng.

- The gathering of Israel—perfecting lives, sharing truth, uniting families, and caring for the poor—is a work of tremendous opportunity and reward.
- Our spiritual foundation needs to be strengthened to cope with unforeseen challenges that will yet confront us.
- Time intentionally spent with the Lord each day is an investment in joy.

This is simply one personal example of offering my time to the Lord. I am profoundly grateful for my forty-day trek that focused my mind and heart on the prophetic voice and gave me renewed determination to be among those who choose to keep in alignment with the living prophet. This is not intended to be easy or convenient. It is instead the high road of discipline and growth. I know that by so doing, great blessings have come into my life and will continue to come into my life.

I had a wonderful spiritual experience as I spent these forty consecutive days listening carefully to the chosen seer of the Lord. I reflected and resolved to align my life more fully with the prophetic declarations He was giving to me. I also received much revelation, inspiration, and encouragement as I engaged in this daily devotion. I testify that the heavens are indeed open in our day. I invite all to have a daily walk with God by heeding the voice of His living servants. I have shared this experience to benefit others. Good news becomes more precious to us as we share it with others! Our faith, testimony, experiences, and knowledge can be a light, example, and hope to others.

Of course, we are not restricted to offering up just our "now" to God. We can, in a sense, offer our past, present, and future to Him also. This is metaphorically like placing a time capsule in the ground to be opened in the future. We offer up our hopes and dreams to God! We place our time on the altar by showing each day that the Lord is important to us. We commit the past to Him by laying our burden at His feet and asking for His forgiveness where needed. We offer up our future to Him by committing now that we will use our future in His service. There is great power in deciding now to live our "tomorrows" unto the Lord.

If we think about the personal and combined offerings of Saints throughout all dispensations—and Latter-day Saints in this final dispensation—we will see literally millions of acts of faith, courage, restraint, dedication, and love being offered in God's cause:

- Millions of hours spent teaching, leading, blessing, ministering, interviewing, listening, and advising
- Millions of hours spent searching God's word
- Millions of hours spent in family history research and temple worship
- Millions of hours spent reaching out to friends to teach restored gospel truths
- Millions of hours spent in fervent prayer and devoted fasting
- Millions of hours spent serving those in need of resources, help, and support

Such hours have been used righteously in the past, are being used to good cause now, and will yet be used in great works in the future. Such hours are like pebbles thrown into water—the ripple effect has impacts far beyond the initial point of contact. The course of the Lord is one eternal round!

The love represented in this wave of righteous offering is significant. The outreach shown in this overflowing effort is remarkable. We cannot possibly fully quantify how much time and effort has been given to the cause of the great latter-day work on both sides of the veil. However, in considering this marvelous work and wonder, we begin to appreciate that this is a Spirit-led labor of love. This offering is especially sublime when it is given freely and without thought of reward. Do we comprehend the magnanimous nature of these hundreds of millions of hours of devoted service?

The Gift of Talents

When I was a very young boy, I was introduced to the film *Superman*, starring Christopher Reeve. I loved the music of the film—it captured the essence of the story so very well. For me, the music has become synonymous with flying in the sky. I associate it with overcoming obstacles, with feeling strong, with making a stand for truth and goodness. It is heroic music for my soul. This beautiful and memorable score was composed by John Williams. I think this movie would not have been as powerful as it was were it not for the perfectly suited music. It was an offering that was commensurate with the great story being told—that to become our best, we must be inspired by a great cause.

The most elevated life can only flow from the deepest truths, from the most profound origins. Our destiny can only truly and fully unfold within the great drama of meaning. It took a composer of the caliber of John Williams to produce an epic score that would correctly reflect the magnificence of Superman at the time and to ensure it would leave a legacy of encouragement and hope for many years to come. Such is what happens when the gifts that God has given to His children are used to reach heights we have never known before. I am so glad that John Williams studied and excelled at music. What if he never did that? My life would have been poorer. His excellent music has enriched me.

Of course, I was also fascinated by the characters. I especially loved Superman. I loved the powers he had! I wanted to fly in the sky, be as strong as steel, fire laser beams from my eyes, walk through fire without being burned, and rescue people from danger. He was my favorite superhero!

As I grew older, I discerned that Clark Kent was not always aware of these abilities nor why he possessed them. Although he had great powers as a child, he did not comprehend the meaning and significance of who he really was and why he had the special gifts he had been given.

The film begins with his father, Jor-El, and his mother, Lara, sending their infant son to earth to prevent his impending death. His father said to him, "You will travel far, my little Kal-El. But we will never leave you. . . . The richness of our lives shall be yours. All that I have, all that I've learned, everything I feel . . . all this and more . . .

I bequeath you, my son. You will carry me inside you all the days of your life. You will make my strength your own and see my life through your eyes, as your life will be seen through mine. The son becomes the father, and the father the son."[5]

Being so young when he traveled to earth, Superman did not know his true origin or destiny as a child. Nor did he know his first parents. As he grew, he felt the frustration of not knowing what to do with his rare gifts. He knew his powers were amazing and impressive, but he felt constrained in using them. He was mistreated by some and felt like an oddball. His adoptive father told him that there was a purpose in having such extraordinary gifts. When his mortal father died suddenly, he felt great sorrow at not being able to save him from death. He had great power but could not save the people he loved.

In his mourning and confusion, the crystal that accompanied him on his voyage directed him on a new path. Although he loved his earthly adoptive mother and was sad to leave her, he knew he needed to find out who he really was. He located a secluded spot in the North and threw the crystal into a body of water. A structure grew that became his new home and served as a tangible reminder of the true home he had left years earlier.

In this "Fortress of Solitude," he received virtual visits from his biological parents who were long since dead but who were then able to instruct him in his identity and mission. He now knew he was Kal-El, son of Jor-El and Lara. For the next twelve years he was educated, trained, and instructed in his true nature and purpose for being. This was a place for him to receive knowledge, comfort, guidance, and reassurance. He learned more about what he was truly capable of and what he could accomplish in helping humanity. In a farewell message, his father said to him, "Live as one of them, Kal-El, to discover where your strength and your power are needed. But always hold in your heart the pride of your special heritage. They can be a great people, Kal-El—they wish to be. They only lack the light to show the way. For this reason above all, their capacity for good, I have sent them you . . .

---

5. *Superman*, directed by Richard Donner (Warner Bros., 1978), https://www.amazon.com/gp/video/detail/B0012QVJXS/ref=atv_dp_share_cu_r.

my only son."[6] This experience would be pivotal in helping him to craft a life of deep purpose and resolve.

When I was a child, I thought that Superman was a great hero because he wanted to help people and was strong and brave. He was impressive to me because of the great powers he had. He was a Superman because he was greater than other men. Of course, there is some merit in this. There are also great lessons here about coming to know that we have great and profound reasons for existing. For example, it was only by going to a place set apart from the world that Superman could receive a clear understanding of who he really was and what his true mission was. He had to come to see his life through the eyes of his first father and mother.

Of course, this story is also limited and even misguided in certain ways. Superman is neither real nor without flaw. In addition, we might incorrectly assume that we must be super special to be important or must be super strong or remarkably fast to be heroic.

While I still love the idea of Superman, I now know that Jesus Christ is a far better example of what it means to be a hero than the fictional Superman. The Savior has knowledge, gifts, talents, strengths, and desires that Superman—even if he were a real person—would not possess. I see shortcomings and weaknesses in Superman that I do not see in Christ. Indeed, our Lord is a hero worthy of perfect admiration.

I believe in God as our literal Father in Heaven. I believe without reservation in Jesus Christ. Our Savior was truly of divine parentage. He came from parents called by the name of El (which means God in Hebrew). He was the Only Begotten of the Father (see 1 Nephi 11:21). Christ traveled far to come to earth in that He condescended to be born as a mortal (see 1 Nephi 11:16). Christ had abilities no other person has ever had, including the power to overcome sin and death for Himself and others (see Alma 7:11–12). Christ developed His comprehension and powers over time and experience, although He evidenced from a remarkably young age that He knew who He was (see Luke 2:52).

---

6. *Superman.*

Christ spent time communing with His Father in Heaven—such as in the temple, in the wilderness for forty days, and on the Mount of Transfiguration—to learn about His likeness to the Almighty and the strong connection they shared. He took time to ponder, reflect, think, pray, and learn—in sacred, holy places—to bring to fruition His divine identity, nature, purpose, and mission. Christ could not do the great work of being an example and Savior to every soul that has ever lived on the earth without first coming to sense deeply His majestic resemblance to the Supreme Being! His goodness stemmed from seeing goodness in His Father and Mother. Our Redeemer came to know by personal experience that He was seen, known, and loved by His Father. He came to see His life through the eyes of His Father. The viewpoint of His Father powerfully inspired Him.

Similarly, each of us needs to know who we are and whose we are. Rather than letting the world teach us who we should be, we need to look to God for instruction and direction. This guidance will be of an eternal nature. It will ring true to us. What is our purpose? We can see our life, at least partially, through the eyes of our Father in Heaven and His Beloved Son. We can learn the divine uses for our already recognized powers. We can then also uncover our hidden gifts, undiscovered talents, and latent potential.

We require time for quiet solace and careful pondering. This is best accomplished in places without noisy and worldly distractions—places where the Holy Ghost can whisper to us, where we can study God's word, and where we can think of things divine. Places of natural scenic beauty work well for me to recharge, renew, and find clear focus again. I especially rejoice in holy places—homes, chapels, and temples—as sacred spaces where I have learned my true nature, identity, purpose, and mission. It makes all the difference in the world to me to see how my Father in Heaven and my Savior see me. I love the precious perspective they offer me! I invite you to have sacred time in a special place to ask God what magnificent possibilities He sees in you. You will not be disappointed!

I also invite you to consider how through coming to know your own light, you will be more empowered to bless others. We cannot possibly love others with the kind of divine love that God requires of us unless we come to see the divinity within them. As we come to see their inner worth, their capacity for goodness, and their potential for greatness, we begin to see them as God does. As we light the world with our gifts, we give encouragement to others to do likewise. We invite them to rise upward to become what they are destined to become. We connect with the light within them and encourage them to increase their divine fire. We give them hope. Our talents will spur them on to belief and action. This is what it means to love others in a Christlike way. It is to call forth the best in others.

As we give God the best of ourselves—our noblest endowments, our greatest abilities, our deepest longings—then we are likewise blessing others in the most beneficial way possible. Our most sublime abilities are God-given, and we cannot possibly have greater gifts or capacities from any other source. Only God can give the greatest gifts! It is also because we are obviously not capable of giving anything more than our ultimate best. Hence, to give our best is an offering that cannot possibly be improved upon—at least in terms of the offering that pertains to that moment where our best shines through. Even our best self can improve over time because our capacity can grow through experience. It is also because we are thereby blessing others to witness the highest good that is in us, and this hopefully will encourage them to do likewise. If they learn to give their best because we inspired them to do so, then surely God will rejoice in both them and us!

This is what the Lord meant when He said we were to love others as we love ourselves. Our creative capacities are to be offered to God in the blessing of our brothers and sisters, whether that involves our knowledge of science, talent in art, or proficiency in a trade or craft. Whether our talents be great or small, they are God-given. Our great privilege is to use them to assist our fellow travelers in the greatest adventure of all—the trek to eternal promise.

The Gift of Treasures

A treasure is something we value highly, something important to us. Imagine what happens to us when we place great value upon our money, cars, houses, stocks, and so on. Imagine then that we offer these up in service of God and our fellow man. If these are great treasures to us and we then use them to serve God and others, isn't that a clear indication that we value God and others as greater treasures than our physical possessions? What a statement that makes to God about how we value Him and our fellow brothers and sisters! We thereby show that we place greater value on God and others than we do on material possessions, titles, or worldly praise. When we give God and others our love, affection, heart, mind, and reputation, we are placing ourselves on the altar. We are choosing to put God first. As the sacred offering of our money is dedicated to the Lord, so likewise our lives become consecrated to God by keeping this standard. Truly, as stewards over earthly blessings, we are accountable to God for what we do with these resources both now and in the next life. Indeed, those who show wisdom through their faithfulness are worthy to inherit mansions in eternity (see Doctrine and Covenants 72:3–4).

God does not want us to cling tenaciously to possessions. He wants us to share them with others: "And now, if God, who has created you, on whom you are dependent for your lives and for all that ye have and are, doth grant unto you whatsoever ye ask that is right, in faith, believing that ye shall receive, O then, how ye ought to *impart of the substance* that ye have one to another" (Mosiah 4:21; emphasis added).

When a prophet-king uses the word "ought," that is a very clear indication of direction! The invitation here makes sense to me. God does not want us to be attached to our material goods. He desires that we use them to bless others. That becomes impossible if we are clinging to them ambitiously. These things can do much good. To impart of them to others is to bestow kindness upon them. It is to treat them the way God treats us, for He truly showers material substance upon us. To impart of what we have is a godly offering we perform in token of God's offerings to us (see Doctrine and Covenants 19:26; 42:31; 88:123; 105:3).

King Benjamin specifically advised his people to use their substance to feed hungry persons, clothe naked souls, and give temporal relief to the sick and those requiring relief from burdens: "And now, for the sake of these things which I have spoken unto you—that is, for the sake of retaining a remission of your sins from day to day, that ye may walk guiltless before God—I would that ye should *impart of your substance* to the poor, every man according to that which he hath, such as feeding the hungry, clothing the naked, visiting the sick and *administering to their relief,* both spiritually and temporally, according to their wants" (Mosiah 4:26; emphasis added). His counsel is likewise extended to us.

I love the idea that our goods are bestowed upon others through love. We endow others with gifts we could have retained for ourselves. This is what it means to impart something to our fellow man that they could not have without our service. It is humbling to bless a soul in need like this. It strikes me as very significant that this process of offering our goods to others in a spirit of Christlike giving will help us walk blameless before God. That is a blessing we dearly need in this world of temptation.

Of course, our treasures are not just material things. Our knowledge is also a great treasure. When we share information, understanding, and insights we have learned with others, we lift them up to where we are. This is a generous gift. We have the riches of revelations! The revelations we have received, both institutionally and personally, have great power to educate, inspire, motivate, uplift, bless, heal, encourage, refine, guide, and assure us. In sharing these revelations with others in appropriate ways, we bless them through the communicating of that which we value deeply. God loves it when we show that our greatest treasures are Him, His ways, and His children.

Those who are striving to be humble, optimistic, cheerful, supportive, gentle, kind, patient, hopeful, concerned, generous, thoughtful, considerate, gracious, caring, diligent, consistent, and persistent are the builders of people, the improvers of relationships, the developers of families, the contributors to communities, and those who bring strength to the Church and kingdom of God on the earth. Such will also be creators of bounty and beauty in heaven, for is not this life the great preparation ground for heaven?

We can catch the vision of the kingdom. Our purpose is to bring true developmental growth and genuine joy to as many people as possible. Our work is to bless individuals with opportunity, challenge, happiness, service, contribution, meaning, purpose, and true fulfillment. The kingdom of God is here on the earth with preparatory power. To belong to it is a great privilege, especially when we sense the prophetic significance of what this means. To build it up and strengthen it in any small way is to literally partake in the work of God. To support it with our time, talents, and treasures is to help prepare for the glorious splendor of that time when the King of kings will dwell among us and abide with us.

9

Give Valued Possessions

Another thing we can offer to God is our most highly regarded possessions—not material things but rather our thoughts, words, and deeds. By offering these for God's use, our souls grow ever closer to the divine ideal.

The most important possessions in our lives are those beliefs that are woven into the very fabric of our souls, the characteristics that are engraven upon our hearts, the attributes that are written in our minds, and the concepts that are embedded in our spirits. They are the values we espouse, the causes we stand for, the ideals we live for, the principles we advocate, and the motives we aspire to when we are living according to our holiest standards. These deeply held viewpoints are both formed and reflected in what we think about, talk about, and do.

King Benjamin gave the Saints in his day firm counsel about examining themselves on an ongoing basis to ensure they were aligned with the directives of God: "But this much I can tell you, that if ye do not *watch* yourselves, and your thoughts, and your words, and your deeds, and observe the commandments of God, and *continue* in the faith of what ye have heard concerning the coming of our Lord, even unto the end of your lives, ye must perish. And now, O man, *remember*, and perish not" (Mosiah 4:30; emphasis added).

If what we are thinking, saying, or doing does not reflect our belief in the Son of God, then it is always beneficial to change our thoughts, words, and actions so they conform to God's ways.

Gift Our Thoughts to God

Thoughts are very important. What we consistently think about shapes us. What others consistently think about shapes them. Thoughts are not disconnected from words and deeds. They influence them and are likewise influenced by them.

I have often thought on the idea of what it means to keep our eyes on the prize. This refers to our target in mind, the object of our focus, the goal we have before us. A basketball player may have great skill and capacity. He may be tall and strong. He may be hardworking and disciplined. He may even be very motivated. This is all necessary, but it is not sufficient. He needs to know one indispensable thing, without which all his ability and training will be essentially fruitless. If he does not remain focused on the primary aim of putting the ball in the net of the other team, he will have no success. If he is not crystal clear about helping his team to score and preventing the other team from scoring, then victory will be quite impossible. He needs to operate both defensively and offensively if he is to triumph.

While the need to focus on scoring might appear obvious, I believe there are times when players become distracted from their core objectives and instead focus primarily on other things—such as their jealousy toward a fellow team player, their animosity toward an opponent, their resistance toward the direction of their coach, their dislike of a decision given by a referee, their arguing with a scorekeeper, their objection to a timekeeper, or their mistrust of a shot clock operator. While these things might encourage one to play better, they might also have the opposite effect. Also, there may be numerous other things going on that impact player performance in negative ways, such as unresolved emotions about a recent breakup, worry about the poor health of a friend, concern over a financial reversal recently experienced, or distress about the recent suicide of a childhood friend. Of course, all these issues are of relevance and importance to them. However, if they allow distraction into their minds arising from these matters, they will find it nearly impossible to keep their focus on the immediate task at hand—that of playing and winning the game. Similarly, a player too focused on the anticipated party after the game might have their attention dominated in a diversionary way.

I often think this kind of thing happens to us in spiritual things. We can very easily get distracted from our ultimate purpose of reaching the celestial kingdom. There are so many potentially derailing things in this world that can distract us from the fundamentals of what God wants us to achieve. Jealousies, regrets, worries, fears, animosities, grudges—and a thousand other variations on those themes—can play a significant part in redirecting our minds and thoughts from where they should be on to other matters of seemingly great import. There are a thousand small diversions that can sap our time and energy. There are problems and issues that can come to control our thinking to the point that spiritual things—the things of real striving—begin to lessen in importance. The real goal of our lives—obtaining celestial living—can be removed from our radar of vital things if we allow ourselves to be swallowed up in the maelstrom of temporary concerns.

Our thoughts can help or hinder us in the spiritual life. The thoughts we focus on shape so much of our experience. Our thoughts about God, ourselves, and others have a huge influence on what we accomplish in life. The gospel invites us to focus on the things that matter to God. It is His perspective that should direct our frame of reference. It is His doctrine that should inform our priorities. Hence, we can ask ourselves:

- Do our thoughts center on the scriptures, righteousness, and the delightful things of the Lord? (see 2 Nephi 4:15–16; Jacob 2:5)
- Do our thoughts evidence a Spirit-led closeness to God? (see Mosiah 5:13; Alma 12:3)

- Are our thoughts reflective of concern for the everlasting well-being of others? (see Mosiah 28:3)
- Are our thoughts focused on defending the holy messengers of God? (see Alma 10:17)
- Do our thoughts commend us to God? (see Alma 12:14)
- Do we think of ways to lead others to believe in Christ? (see Alma 17:30)
- Do we think on our freedoms, liberties, lands, families, and religion? (see Alma 43:48)

Alma gives us great counsel to direct our thoughts to God: "Yea, and cry unto God for all thy support; yea, let all thy doings be unto the Lord, and whithersoever thou goest let it be in the Lord; yea, let all thy thoughts be directed unto the Lord; yea, let the affections of thy heart be placed upon the Lord forever" (Alma 37:36; emphasis added).

The word "let" implies that we need to allow this process to unfold against the backdrop of likely resistance. I believe that the overarching teaching of the Lord concerning our thoughts is that we should use them to draw ourselves and others closer to God. As we intentionally think of God more, incline our hearts toward our Father in Heaven, and ponder on our Savior, our thoughts gravitate upward. They become richer, more refined, more holy. As we think more on Christ, we will encourage others to do likewise. This gift of giving our thought patterns to God more fully will please Him.

Gift Our Words to God

Words matter. What we say has a significant impact on both ourselves and others. Our framing of concepts has a marked impact on our lives. Words paint images in our minds, help us recall past memories, stir up emotions, and point us to future possibilities. The mere mention of particular words can shape our moods:

- Scary words—terror, horror, dread, and anxiety. Such words conjure up a measure of fearful worry.
- Reassuring words—bliss, delight, beauty, and peace. Such words engender serenity.

- Empowering words—inspire, move, calm, and edify. Such words encourage renewed determination, hope, and vigor.

Our employment of words can do much to sustain the cause of Christ. Consider the following.

Teaching words—Enos was taught about eternal life through the words of his father Jacob (see Enos 1:3).

Healing words—Jacob refers to the pleasing word of God that heals the wounded soul (see Jacob 2:8). Alma explains that he was loosed from the pains of hell by the power of God's words.

Comforting words—Emma Smith reassured her husband Joseph with comforting words (see Doctrine and Covenants 25:5).

Warning words—Our words can condemn us (see Alma 12:14). This happens when we use words in self-indicting ways. Our words can reveal our wickedness to the world.

Protecting words—The revelations concerning the last days tell us to treasure the words of God so that we might avoid the deception of our adversary and his cunning emissaries (see Joseph Smith—Matthew 1:37).

Edifying words—Words can be used to inspire people to greater holiness (see Doctrine and Covenants 136:24).

Powerful words—Nephi refers to the sharpness of the power of the word of God (see 2 Nephi 1:26). Alma teaches that pride can be pulled down by God's word (see Alma 4:19) and that the word of God leads people to act justly (see Alma 31:5). The revelations declare that the word of God is mighty (see Helaman 10:5). We can be delivered from various types of enemies by God's word (see 3 Nephi 28:20).

Miraculous words—All things were created by God's word (see Mormon 8:33). A sea was parted (see 1 Nephi 17:26–31), miracles were wrought (see Mormon 9:17), and both humans and the earth trembled (see Moses 6:47; 7:13) when the word of God was involved.

Promising words—The word of God cannot pass away (see 2 Nephi 9:16), does not pass away (see Mormon 8:33), is sure (see Doctrine and Covenants 64:31), and is compared to an iron rod (see 1 Nephi 11:5). The words of God are not fickle or trivial. They have enduring power and validity.

It is useful therefore for us to consciously employ the word of God in these ways. As we do so, we find that we are blessed and others are uplifted and guided.

The couching of an idea in gospel words can do much to foster spiritual growth. It can also be detrimental if we locate spiritual notions in primarily worldly terms. I often find that a shift in language can lead to a marked improvement in our efforts to become perfect in our Savior. Let us consider how word choice can shape our spiritual lives in essential ways. Comparing words and their associated connotations can help us in offering the best gifts.

Volunteering or Covenant Discipleship?

I have noticed the increasing use of the word "volunteer" in church settings. While I understand that we want to encourage people to opt in for service rather than feeling obligated or overburdened, I worry that "volunteering" is not really a scriptural concept—it's more of a social construct. The scriptures do not talk about Jehovah volunteering to be our Savior. They talk about Him accepting the plan of the Father and desiring to bring it to fruition, even at great personal cost to Himself. While He did say, "Here am I, send me" (Abraham 3:27), and this is certainly a free will offering, it is not precisely analogous to the modern equivalent of volunteering, which reflects willingness without pay or conscription. I admit there is something of that notion in the Savior's willingness to perform a duty voluntarily, but His statement strikes me as more binding and serious than a simple statement of volunteering.

When I hear the word *volunteer*, I think of opting in or opting out depending on what suits us. It seems like a very casual proposal. A volunteer can change his or her mind, make a promise and then not keep it, give up on a task they regard as more difficult than they bargained for initially, or give excuses for why it is no longer possible for them to do a given task. I am not suggesting that volunteering is bad or that all volunteers lack commitment. Nor do I mean that it is never appropriate to opt out of volunteering if personal circumstances make it difficult or impossible to continue. However, the connotation for me is associated with doing something primarily because the volunteer chooses to do it rather than because they have been asked to do it or because they have given their word or made a promise. Volunteering is commendable. However, the efforts of volunteers are only as reliable as their character. Promises easily made are easily broken, neglected, or forgotten.

I prefer to think of myself as a covenant disciple. I choose to follow Christ. I like to follow Him. My covenants are not casual. They are sacred to me. My Lord is sacred to me. I love Him and want to follow Him. I believe couching our discipleship in terms of covenants gives a sense of devotion and permanence to our responsibilities that the notion of volunteering does not. Volunteering does not require covenants. It does not require the kind of deep-seated dedication that lifelong belonging to Christ does. This is especially important when we are called to serve by the Lord. Such service opportunities are usually quite onerous. To serve others as Christ would implies that we are going to face times when such service requires us to dig really deep. To offer a gift to Christ like the wise men did will require far more than a willingness to volunteer. It will require us to travel far through all the seasons of life in a spirit of deep devotion.

Hardship or Opportunity?

To think of every sacrifice, difficulty, and trial purely in terms of how hard, inconvenient, or demanding it is results in seeing only some elements of the task. It is to paint it in bleak terms. It is a little self-pitying, as if all we ever experience is trouble. Opportunity, on the other hand, suggests adventure, learning, contribution, growth, and worthwhile endeavors. It shows that God rewards us in addition to asking something from us. This is more hopeful than thinking our lives are all about tribulation.

Suffering or Mellowing?

Only focusing on suffering makes us see only our trials and difficulty. It indicates pain, misery, inconvenience, and sorrow. I think it is better to refer to "mellowing" because this suggests we are going through something so that we become something more. We are to be refined. We are to be softened, strengthened, and made better. It showcases that God is not a cruel tyrant seeking to inflict punishment on us. He is seeking our improvement. We gain by suffering if we allow it to make us kinder, wiser, more pliant, and more humble.

"Have to" or "Choose to"?

"Have to" sounds compelled, forced, and strained. "Choose to" sounds much more hopeful because it is grounded in volition. It is active, deliberate, conscientious, and considered. It is a sign we are involved, active, and invested. It promotes engagement. It gives us a sense of power and triumph rather than powerlessness and defeat.

We can take this approach with so many things in life, including the gospel. As we reframe our decisions in terms of God's paradigm, we are much more likely to endure with optimistic joy. We will still have much trouble, but we will be masters of our words instead of them controlling us. Our words will promote faith, encourage determination, build resilience, and engender love. Others will be inspired by our language to come unto Christ. Such use of language is a gift we can offer to God and His children. I trust that we will have opportunities to impart the word of God to others in ways that will bless them in time and eternity with peace, love, knowledge, joy, and salvation (see Mosiah 28:1; Alma 16:14).

Gift Our Deeds to God

Many years ago I worked with a woman who liked to talk. She was especially open about her personal life. She may have deeply trusted me, or perhaps her need to talk was so great that she was willing to talk about her troubles to anyone. She regularly conversed with me about her husband. She explained that he had many shortcomings. She said that she had confronted him numerous times about his failings in the marriage. His response had been, "I am aware of that deficiency." Apparently, at least from her account of how these communications went, her husband felt that his response was sufficient. In other words, he felt that once he was aware of how his wife felt and he acknowledged to her the genuine nature of her concern, the matter was concluded.

She responded to him by saying that such awareness was necessary but not sufficient. She wanted him to change his behavior. She wanted him to act differently. For her it was not enough to just recognize a fault—it was imperative to do something to change it. I could see the rationale in her thinking. She was asserting that true love in relationships involves more than the recognition of a problem. There must be action taken to remedy the problem. I believe she was correct. Her husband was either unaware or unwilling to change. Clearly, the relationship was essentially locked into a stalemate of inaction. I suppose little has changed in the relationship since that time, although it is entirely possible that the relationship has broken down to the point of being impossible to repair. I think most reasonable people would say that listening in relationships is not enough—there must also be action taken to resolve difficulties. This is on the assumption that improvement is desired.

It is important to note that this good lady was not without her own shortcomings. In our conversations, she rarely if ever acknowledged to me any behavior on her part that was lacking. If she was aware of any such shortcomings in her own performance, she certainly did not discuss any efforts to address them. We can become so preoccupied with the perceived limitations of others that we become immune to detecting our own. She never asked me to advise her on whether I thought she could approach things differently with her husband for a better potential outcome. Her interest seemed to be in announcing his demonstrable faults with which she was becoming increasingly frustrated and despairing.

The main point of this little story is that intentions, attitudes, and aspirations are not enough. We must determine to act in our lives if we want to make things happen. I suspect that each of us could do with an increase in introspection, objective perspective, and willingness to improve ourselves. While this couple were not members of the Church, it is evident that their behaviors were greatly impacting their marriage and family life in negative ways. Church members are not immune from the responsibility to work out our salvation.

The works, actions and behaviors of our lives make a difference. They are significant. In our desires to become perfect in Christ, the deeds we perform either lead us to Him more fully or lead us away from Him. Likewise, our deeds lead others to Him or away from Him. Especially in these days of division, we are increasingly being confronted with the stark choice to follow the gospel way or some other way. One of the gifts we give to God and others is our willingness to overcome our own bad behaviors and develop good ones. Likewise, assisting others to overcome their weaknesses is a gift to them.

So we might fruitfully ask ourselves, "What kind of behavior am I exhibiting?" Consider the differences between the left and right sides of this table:

Covenant lifting that holds to high personal standards and strives to become a better disciple of Christ	Casual leaning that is content with mediocre performance, minimum standards, plateau resting, or trying to be more worldly
Rejoices in the successes of others, quick to see good in others, encourages others to be faithful, acts to build and strengthen the kingdom of God through loyalty	Jealous of the accomplishments of others, quick to see faults in others, entices others to be faithless, acts to weaken and tear down the kingdom of God through disloyalty
Studious, prayerful, obedient, diligent, faithful, loving, serving, humble, courageous, submissive, believing, hardworking	Complacent, non-devotional, disobedient, carefree, sporadic, antagonistic, selfish, proud, fearful, rebellious, doubting, lazy

I have walked the line between both these types of living. I have at times been mixed in my discipleship. However, as I have matured, I have inclined more in the direction of covenant faithfulness. I have gradually become much better in my capacity to be my better, nobler self. It is important to introspectively reflect on ourselves and to call ourselves out for times when we falter. This can be done in gentle ways so that we do not lose love for ourselves (see Doctrine and Covenants 121). This is an act of self-love—a moment of self-improvement. The recognition of failing can be an opportunity for growth.

Trust Our Thoughts, Words, and Deeds to God

I have often reflected on the account of Peter the Apostle leaping from the boat into the tempestuous sea to approach the Savior (see Mark 14:24–33). As far as I can tell, it is the only scriptural account of a human being walking on water. We are all aware that he began to sink when the winds became boisterous. However, it is significant to note that he did walk successfully for a portion of time. This is of tremendous import. The implications are stunning. Peter had at least a portion of faith. He did walk—on water. A man of mortal flesh walked on a liquid substance as if it had been solid ground. I believe the idea is that Christ changes our foundation from shifting to secure, from dangerous to safe, from precarious to wonderful. He makes otherwise impossible things not only possible but normal.

When Peter subsequently faltered, he was reminded by the Lord that it is possible for humans to have faith in the Lord. Indeed, the Savior expects us to have such faith in Him. The suggestion from the words of Jesus to Peter is that Peter would have continued to walk on the water through sufficient faith in the Lord. He would not have faltered or sunk. He would not have given way to fear. To lose one's focus on the Lord is to lose security, to be diminished in protection, to find strong reason to doubt and fear. To give credence to the storms of life is to give them more power than they need to have. To believe—and continue to believe—in the Son of God will assure us safe passage through all the vicissitudes of mortal life.

Peter could have kept walking on the water. He started right and could have continued going in that manner. He could have prevailed without the need for immediate and urgent rescue. This is not to suggest that he could walk on water alone. He could walk because he believed in the Son of God. When he gave his concentration and attention to the waves of turbulence rather than Christ, then his foundation changed from strong to weak, from certain to tentative. He was overpowered and overcome.

The lessons of this incident are many and they are pivotal. Let us go on in the faith that compelled us forward in the first instance. Walking on water is possible. So is healing the sick, deaf, blind, and maimed. So is raising the dead. So is seeing angels. So is having revelation. So are a thousand other things that the everlasting gospel promises. To the world, these things are foolish and impossible. To the natural man or woman, these things are ridiculous. To the purely rational person, these things are illogical. However, to the man or woman of faith in Christ, these things are not only normal but are in truth inevitable. As we shift our thinking from the carnal confines of a momentary world, we are free to believe that which is the everyday walk of angels and gods.

In God's goodness, He gives us the scope to choose the possessions of soul that come to be the most valued parts of our lives. I am convinced that as we come to dedicate these personal possessions to God, we will come to know richness beyond compare. As we direct our thoughts, words, and deeds to the uplifting of the human family, we will come to know the approbation of heaven in a sweet, personal way.

10

Show Noble Signs

Similar to the tokens I spoke about earlier, there are also signs we can give to God to indicate we are paying careful attention to Him. Here I will highlight the three signs of hallowing the Sabbath day, having high regard for the temple, and reverencing divine names. I believe we can learn nobility of soul by responding conscientiously to these core aspects of our covenant life.

Show Signs of Honoring the Sabbath Day

The Sabbath was instituted by God for man. It is an edifying truth that originates with God. The Sabbath enables us to become more like God. Hence, it allows us to prepare to enter back into His presence in due course. Indeed, careful attention to Sabbath day observance is necessary for our salvation in the celestial kingdom of heaven.

We are commanded to rest from temporal labors on the Sabbath. However, we are not commanded to rest from any spiritual labors on that day! In fact, we are invited to "do well" on that special day. Man does not live by temporal bread alone but by every word that God speaks. While physical bread sustains the mortal body, only spiritual food in the form of God's marvelous word sustains the eternal spirit.

God does not want us to starve spiritually, nor to be malnourished through lack of hearing His word. He wants to share His word with us, especially on the holy day, so that we may live spiritually.

The resting of the Lord on the seventh day makes great sense to me. Why? It is because we are instructed to enter the rest of the Lord (see Doctrine and Covenants 84:24), meaning His presence or the fullness of His glory. The Sabbath is the great day of spiritual rest. In other words, the seventh day is symbolically representative of the rest, or presence of, the Lord. The fact that the Sabbath day was blessed and sanctified by the Lord shows that we too can be blessed and sanctified by the Lord because of our observance of that day. Think of the sacrament prayers as blessing prayers (see Doctrine and Covenants 20:77–79). The Sabbath day is a day of sanctification to those who partake of it in the way designated by God. Indeed, those observing the Sabbath day symbolically and even literally on occasion enter God's divine presence on that day.

The Sabbath is for developing and evidencing our devotion to God. Indeed, showing an interest in, and dedication to, godly things on the Sabbath reflects willingness, knowledge, and obedience on our part in alignment with the purpose of the day. Only through full devotion to God can we obtain the complete blessings of Sabbath worship. The level of attention we give to God and His holy work on the Sabbath day is a clear indication of how spiritual we are becoming.

If we will go to church on the Lord's day and partake of prayer and the sacrament, then we will be more fully unspotted from the world. Think of that for a moment. Our very capacity to resist evil and have spiritual purity in our lives is directly related to church attendance in a spirit of humility and penitence. Worship is good for the soul! Conscientious observance of the Sabbath is both an indicator of personal desire to be clean and one of the core ways we acquire further purification of our lives.

The Sabbath is a day for conversing with Deity. This allows us to know God more fully. Indeed, the sacramental prayer reflects the very purpose for which the Sabbath was given. It is the day we remember the pierced body and the shed blood of our Savior Jesus Christ. That remembrance is not a small or insignificant thing. Remembering Him is powerful. It connects us to Him in profound ways. It changes the thinking and relating patterns of our lives. To remember backward is also to imagine forward. This connective tissue that binds us to Him in a deeply personal way influences all our most important decisions and relationships. His bruising heals us. How? Well, priesthood holders ask, on our behalf, for the bread and the water, which represent His body and blood respectively, to be blessed and sanctified to us. This is how we ask God to bless and sanctify our souls, through the sacrificial offering of Christ. It is also a way of showing our acceptance of the Resurrection of Christ from the dead. We pledge our loyalty to Christ by promising to always immerse ourselves through our covenants in the character of Christ. This is how we bind ourselves to the Lord and obtain the blessing of having His spirit with us always.

The sacramental prayer begins with the words "O God, the Eternal Father, we ask thee in the name of thy Son, Jesus Christ" (Doctrine and Covenants 20:77). These words suggest an implicit acceptance on our part of the doctrine of the divine sonship of Christ. This powerful truth is plainly manifest through symbolism. Christ not only died but was "born again" to a newness of resurrected life—a life far more magnificent than mortality could ever be, even for Him. The Resurrection literally indicates that Christ is the Only Begotten of the Father after the manner of the flesh. Thus, Christ is the literal true and living Son of the literal true and living Father. To reflect on the resurrected Christ on the Sabbath is to recall His being in the express image of His Father.

The sacramental prayer allows us to witness before our Father in Heaven that we are willing to take upon ourselves the name of Christ, to always remember Him, and to keep His commandments. This means that we evidence our desire to become like Christ by making a covenant to be yoked, bound, and consecrated to Him. We make this covenant of consecration newly each Sunday. The very fact that we remember this important day shows that we are thinking on our baptismal and sacramental promises. We have not forgotten. Or, if we have forgotten, we are calling ourselves to repentance. To remember to keep the Sabbath day holy, sacred, and pure is to both understand and fulfill the very purpose for which it was given to us. Perpetual remembrance of God is highlighted on this sacred day.

We are commanded to glorify God on the Sabbath. Thus, we should praise God on this day. We are to rejoice in Him, to honor and thank Him. We subscribe to His work and glory by doing those things that prepare us for eternal life with Him. We give ourselves to everlasting life in the eternities by accepting gladly and completely the Lord Jesus Christ now. Our yielding to Him is shown in our sincere efforts to become more like Him. Indeed, the true way to truly glorify God is to imitate His nature.

Our vows are to be offered up in righteousness on the Sabbath (see Doctrine and Covenants 59:11–12). Our dedication to the Lord is shown by our acting in righteousness or "rightness" on His holy day. In effect, our offerings are to be done in the right manner and in the right attitude. Particularly, we are to worship in the name of Jesus Christ (the correct manner) and with a pure desire to emulate the attributes of our Savior (the proper attitude). Our oblations are to be given to the Lord on this day. Hence, our time, talents, and means are to be used to serve God and our fellow men and women on the Sabbath. Our loyalty to God is shown by, and developed through, our righteous service to God and His children on the Lord's Day. We are to confess our sins on the Sabbath. We honestly admit our weaknesses while simultaneously expressing a heartfelt desire to overcome those shortcomings with the help of God. Thus, the Sabbath allows us to reconcile ourselves with the Lord and His divine will for our lives.

We are commanded to have "singleness of heart" on the Sabbath so that our fasting may be perfect or so that our joy may be full. This means, I think, that a pure heart will enable us to hunger and thirst after righteousness with total longing. Our joy will likewise know completion. Significantly, the extent to which we seek to be righteous on the Sabbath will be the level to which we find joy. Goodness is happiness. Indeed, the Sabbath is the chosen day upon which we draw closest to fulfilling our divinely appointed purpose of finding and having true joy in life. The sacramental prayers clearly specify that we will always have the Holy Spirit to be with us if we keep our sacramental covenants. Similarly, the constant companionship of the Spirit is the inevitable blessing that comes to those who accept the doctrine of the divine sonship of our Lord and who embrace Christlike character through covenant action.

Of great importance is the truth that the great revelation that came to John the Revelator rested upon him while he was "in the spirit on the Lord's Day" (Revelation 1:10). Receiving the association of the Spirit leads to gaining profound knowledge and guidance from God. Likewise, if we seek to do the Lord's will on the Sabbath rather than anything else, then the Lord will be pleased with us. He will lead us, instruct us, reveal Himself to us, and care for us. We will find deep happiness in worshipping God. What majestic promises are these!

Jesus Christ is truly the Lord of the Sabbath. To observe the holy day properly is to worship the Lord of that day. Those who do so have more than knowledge about Christ—they know Him. They are His disciples, and He is their Lord and Master. To freely give one day per week to let our thoughts and actions be swallowed up in loving and serving Him is a marvelous sign we can give to God of our deep regard for him!

Give Signs of Temple Worship

I often think about the story of *A Christmas Carol* by Charles Dickens. I think it offers much hope and encouragement. It inspires me to be a better man. I watch a version of it at least once each Christmas season, and it never fails to touch my heart. I love the way Ebenezer Scrooge gets the opportunity to change his life. Very few people think there is any hope for him. Only his nephew Fred and his employee Bob Cratchit seem to think there is hope for him and treat him kindly. Even the ghosts that visit him are quite antagonistic. Perhaps that is the only language Scrooge will understand given his long entrenchment in miserly materialism.

However, there is one aspect of the story that has always bothered me. It centers around Jacob Marley. While Scrooge gets the opportunity for redemption, Jacob Marley never does. This is obviously an outgrowth of the prevailing theological perspective at the time—that individuals who die in their sins are eternally bound to sorrow. This is a very bleak and depressing picture. We know that the restored gospel gives us a much more hopeful outlook for the deceased spirits who pass from this life who are willing and able to change in the world of spirits. Temple work is founded on the justice and mercy of God. It offers salvation to those who did not have an opportunity for the sacred work while in the body. While I do not believe that the stubborn and resistant will automatically or easily change their desires and inclinations in the spirit world (see Alma 34), it is evident that temple work helps captive spirits to find escape from their bondage of sin (see Doctrine and Covenants 138). In this sense, the Prophet Joseph Smith was far more inspired than Charles Dickens was.

By the standard of justice alone, it makes little sense to offer Ebenezer Scrooge salvation while refusing the opportunity to Jacob Marley. This is especially the case because Scrooge lived in wretchedness seven years longer than Marley! In addition, Marley showed signs of deep remorse as evidenced by his coming to offer a way out of wickedness to his business associate in the flesh. While this was a form of obligatory penitence for Marley, there also seems to be an element of concern that his friend should not suffer a similar fate to himself. In this sense, the story of *A Christmas Carol* has a measure of truth associated with it—it just does not have the breadth and depth of Christianity that the restored gospel has. I do not blame Dickens for this, as the knowledge of the redemption from the dead was unknown to him. However, the Restoration clearly improves on the usual story of God's justice and mercy by bringing both into perfect equilibrium through the ordinances and covenants of the temple.

I would love to see a new version of the story where Jacob and his fellow lost souls had the opportunity to find salvation. If they were willing, they might be saved. By doing temple work, we are administering the very justice and mercy of God. I rejoice that all human beings will have the opportunity to learn that God will save us to the extent we are willing to be saved. He is not a capricious God. His work proves His love. Likewise, our temple service is a blessing and a gift that we scarcely comprehend in glory and scope. Let us consider what our temple work signifies to God and our brothers and sisters in the world of spirits, and by extension to the living mortal souls we invite to partake in God's temple ordinances.

What sign does our temple service give to the Lord? How is it an offering to Him? Well, there is the great preparation required. To go to the temple requires much effort. We need to learn to conform our lives to divine standards. This is not easy. We participate in temple preparation classes. We pay attention to financial preparation because it costs money to travel to the temple. We confess our serious sins to priesthood leaders. We get our spiritual houses in order. We do this again and again until we are ready. We are made better by this sacred preparation.

In temple service, we offer our lives to God's work. In addition, we search out the names of our ancestors and provide vicarious ordinances on their behalf. The Lord loves it when we do things that bless the lives of others. He loves the fact that we are thinking about our forebears. This unselfish service is a blessing to many others. We take time from our busy lives to do temple work for each person in our family tree—one by one. We focus on the one. We save that which is lost. We seek to rescue those who cannot rescue themselves. That is a work in token of the Atonement of Christ. Our service is a clear sign to the Lord that we value what He values, that we think about what He thinks about, that we are concerned with the souls of our loved ones.

Temple ordinances have the potential to be genuinely life-renewing to both mortals and departed spirits:

- Baptism is a new birth.
- Confirmation is a fresh start.
- Initiatory is a holy transformation.
- Endowment is an awakened commencement.
- Sealing begins a changed life.

These blessings don't just apply to us in mortality. They also represent a new beginning in the world of spirits. The eyes of the spirits who are gone ahead are opened, their ears unstopped, their hearts refreshed, and they can soar to new places, new heights, and new vistas. As the prophet Nephi learned marvelous wonders on a high mountain, so can we do likewise as we deliberately ponder over God's ordinances, covenants, plans, promises, and word. We can seek His counsel and pursue His understanding.

The temple is a fountain of healing. What of the blind, deaf, lame, and diseased? The temple ordinances give them a form of sight, sound, capacity, and healing. These "new" revelations of the temple both surprise and comfort us. The temple gives us enhancement, newness, improvement. Our bodies and spirits are made better. These great blessings apply both to the living and the departed who receive them. They are given a new spiritual life by accepting revealed truth and obtaining divine ordinances. In that sense, we become saviors on Mount Zion when we offer these marvelous covenants to those who have passed on. This is how we make the full redemptive, protective, and enabling powers of Jesus Christ available to those we love in the spirit world. This vicarious offering gives full effect to the atoning sacrifice of Christ across time and space. What a labor of love this is. Gifts, powers, and cleansing are thereby made available to all souls.

Let us ponder how academic processions for conferral of university degrees is a secular form of temple worship, and how the invitation to enter the house of the Lord is an opportunity to be enlisted in the royal citizenship of the kingdom of God. First, consider the format of a graduation ceremony:

- The wearing of robes and caps is essential.
- Tests and exams must be passed and validated.
- Candidates are presented for awards of distinction.
- There is a convocation of like-minded individuals in the company of family and friends. It is presided over by those in authority.
- There is an orderly procession where beautiful music is played. A sense of dignity prevails.
- Individuals present themselves before officials.

- There is the granting of an accredited award—a certificate bearing the "seal" of the university.
- There are congratulations and celebrations, and instruction and advice is given by university representatives.
- Awarded candidates are now empowered to use official designations of qualifications after their names.
- This is seen as a qualification for entry into employment and further levels of study.
- Graduating candidates wear black or red gowns.

Now consider the format of the temple ceremony. The similarities are instructive and inspiring:

- We are clothed in white.
- We are tried and tested at each stage of our progression.
- We come to receive gifts of special knowledge.
- There is a convening and a meeting of like-minded souls. Everything is led by one who is commissioned.
- Peaceful music and orderly procession prevail.
- Officials commit or bestow knowledge to each person.
- Special instruction is received and rewards given.
- Participants are welcomed and honored, and counsel is given.
- Those who complete the course of instruction are so designated on the records of the Church.
- This achievement prepares the way for further knowledge and opportunity.
- Candidates are dressed in white robes that God recognizes as kingly and queenly. We are washed white in the blood of the Lamb. Sin and death can have no permanent hold on those upon whom the Lord Jesus Christ has placed His name and seal.

Thus it is that we receive a royal conferral in the house of the King. We are being inducted into the way of Christ in a deeper and more significant way than ever before. This is a necessary precursor to that which lies ahead in the celestial kingdom of our God.

It is therefore no wonder that God tells us to bring our greatest treasures to the house of covenants. In a revelation on the building of a holy temple in this dispensation, the Lord instructed Joseph Smith to "send ye swift messengers, yea, chosen messengers, and say unto them: Come ye, with all your gold, and your silver, and your precious stones, and with all your antiquities; and with all who have knowledge of antiquities, that will come, may come, and bring the box tree, and the fir tree, and the pine tree, together with all the precious trees of the earth" (Doctrine and Covenants 124:26).

In other words, our greatest treasures should be brought to the temple. Obviously, this refers to material treasures to beautify the house of God. However, I believe there are even greater riches than these. I believe that trees are a great symbol of the children of God. We are trees in the garden of the Lord when we grow to a great stature in God. We are the precious trees He wants brought to His garden place—his temple of Eden. He wants us to bring our families and friends—great trees in His green field—souls to come to His holy house. He wants us to bring the names of those who are passed to the spirit world—special trees in His forest—beings to be given access to His house of prayer. Let us bring the most important riches to His house: our fellow brothers and sisters.

Display Signs of Reverence for Divine Names

Why should the name of God be hallowed? Why is it forbidden to use God's name in vain? Many reasons could be given. I will address just a few.

First, God's name is holy and sacred. As the Supreme Being, He is the highest, noblest, greatest being of whom we have any knowledge. His attributes are perfect. In all ways, God is magnificent. Speaking with regard, deference, respect, and care about Him is perfectly consistent with the truth of His marvelous nature.

Second, to use His name in vain can have several meanings. It can mean to use His name in a blasphemous way. This is to disregard or defile His name and hence His character, His work, and His plans. To speak in a crass, polluted, or denigrating way about Him is to represent that which is beautiful in an ugly way. It is to refer to sacred things in a profane manner. It can also mean using His name in a self-serving way. This can include priestcraft, which is where men promote their own popularity, gifts, and abilities instead of encouraging others to look to God. This is vain in the sense of self-seeking. It involves the use of words, ideas, clothing, and so on to convince others to follow a man, woman, or institution concerned with their own praise and glory rather than persuading others to come to Christ.

Finally, using the name of God in vain can indicate that it has been used without authority, without sanction, or without permission. This is what happens when men claim to speak in the name of God or perform His works without being duly commissioned to do so. To claim to represent God without having been properly designated by Him is a most serious matter—especially when done with insidious intent. Doing good is proper, but if we are claiming to act in the name of God, it is vital that we are called by Him and have His permission. Otherwise, there will be no saving power in what we teach and the ordinances we perform. When it comes to authorizing and performing saving ordinances, any claim of acting in the name of God must be in legitimate alignment with His directives and approval.

It is significant to note that all these uses are "vain" in the sense that they lack the power of God. When God gives authority to men and women to perform a work, He has given them both sanction and capacity. He has given them influence and capability. That power is the power to save souls. In other words, it is the power to lead people to Christ. Christ saves. His name saves. His servants use His name and the name of the Father to bring men to salvation. For example, the scriptures of our day teach "that as many as would believe and be baptized in his holy name, and endure in faith to the end, should be saved" (Doctrine and Covenants 20:25). Teaching about Christ is always intended to lead others to partake of ordinances and enter covenants. It is anticipated that such persons will remain in covenant faithfulness eternally and be saved in God's highest heaven if they do so. This is a chief purpose of the name of God.

Anything that does not concern true salvation is not in alignment with God's name. His name is salvific. His servants seek to save. If God's name is used in a way that does not save those who qualify for salvation, then it is being used in vain. For example, the use of foul language does not edify, enlighten, or inspire; rather, it corrupts. The adversary uses the name of God in vain, having neither authority nor righteousness in so doing. His desire is to prevent our salvation. God, on the other hand, uses His holy name to save our souls. I rejoice when the name of God is upheld, honored, sustained, and respected.

What about our own names? What's in a name? Well, the doctrine of names is that they reflect our mission, work, and efforts on the earth. To honor our name is no small thing. To know our name, reverence it, remember it, and magnify it is a quest of a lifetime.

The name "Thomas" is often treated poorly—the phrase "doubting Thomas" is one we hear often. Obviously, this derives from the scriptural account of the Apostle Thomas. He said he would not believe that Christ was risen unless and until he saw Him and touched the prints of the nails in His hands. Thomas had heard the witness of others who saw the risen Christ, but he was not ready to believe. The Savior said to him, "Thomas, because thou hast seen me, thou hast believed: blessed are they that have not seen, and yet have believed" (John 20:29). It is evident here that the Savior placed a premium on having a believing disposition. The Lord was not impressed by the idea that physical proof precedes belief or that we have a right to demand visual evidence from God before accepting the miraculous.

This does not mean that the Lord does not want to appear to us in person. It does not mean that there is no merit in seeing divine miracles with our actual eyes. It does not even mean that the Lord will not reveal Himself to us if we demand proof in advance of believing. However, it clearly does mean that "believing and seeing" in that order is preferable to "seeing and believing." I hope that Thomas learned the lesson being taught and remedied his perspective so that going forward he was willing to accept the word and witness of reliable testators prior to seeing miracles. There is great wisdom in adopting this viewpoint.

Would Thomas the Apostle have expressed the initial viewpoint he did if he knew that his name would be automatically linked with disbelief in the written record of the Bible for millennia to come? Possibly not. Although it makes the account more authentic, it is not very likely that Thomas wanted his legacy of remembrance to be based on a potentially embarrassing personal difficulty in believing the miracle of the Resurrection without seeing it first. This gives us all a great way of measuring in advance what we want to be known and remembered for as the dominant perspectives of our lives.

I also think it's unfortunate that the Apostle Thomas has thereafter been associated with doubt, as if that is the only attribute he ever possessed. I am not entirely sure that this word fully describes his posture at the time, and I certainly hope it did not describe his approach after the event of witnessing the risen Lord. Doubt generally tends to connote disbelief, incredulity, and resistance. Of course, militant doubt is far more problematic than having curiosity, questions, and tentative confusions that may still lend themselves to moving forward. Clearly, there are degrees of doubt, and some forms are more difficult to resolve than others.

On a more fundamental level, I believe Thomas did become a loyal witness of the risen Lord. There is, in that sense, great hope for all of us who may have had trouble believing wonderful things prior to experiencing them personally. So whatever the exact categorization of his difficulty, it appears he rose above his trouble and bore faithful witness throughout the remainder of his life.

The name "Thomas" means twin in Aramaic. Who was Thomas the twin of? Did he have a brother? Was he like unto his Lord? In my view, he was to be a twin to God—trying to mirror divine attributes in His countenance. Thomas also connotes the idea of leadership. Who did he lead? He led people to Christ!

Nevertheless, not every person with the same name possesses the same attributes. So although Thomas did initially doubt, obviously not everyone named Thomas is a doubter of spiritual things. We ought not to let our names confine us to the replication of bad behaviors attributed to those who held the name before us.

I love the name Thomas. It is my name. I value it highly. I hope to honor it and magnify it. I hope it is associated with respect, admiration, and noble qualities. I hope my name is aligned with righteous ways. I hope to be a leader "like unto" the Lord. This is not about status, aspiration, or ambition but rather about the earnest desire to emulate Christlike qualities and encourage others to follow the Son of God. The name Thomas becomes elevated through the incorporation of qualities associated with the Savior Jesus Christ.

In giving our name and reputation to the Lord, we turn something very precious to us over to Him for His profound and powerful uses. For example, President Thomas S. Monson expressed His desire to be an instrument in the Lord's hands. "The sweetest experience I know in life is to feel a prompting and act upon it and later find out that it was the fulfillment of someone's prayer or someone's need," he said. "And I always want the Lord to know that if He needs an errand run, Tom Monson will run that errand for Him."[7]

In similar fashion, each of us can take upon ourselves the name and character of Christ. My point is that we can look to the best version of our names and seek to rise to the noble side of them.

For example, I have great respect for Elder D. Todd Christofferson. What a marvelous last name! Christ—offer—son. Indeed, as the Son of God, Christ was the offering of the Father to the rest of us. Surely Elder Christofferson has taken upon himself the name of his Lord—in a very literal way! In this sense, names can and do point us to what can be the sweetest blessings in time and eternity! So what is in a name? So very much. I invite you to let your name be associated with all that is good and wonderful about you, your family, and especially your Lord and God.

I am profoundly grateful to know that by our focus on these three great signs—honoring the Sabbath, worshipping in the temple, and revering divine names—we can show the Lord of life that we love Him and our brothers and sisters everywhere and all the time.

---

7. Thomas S. Monson, quoted in William R. Walker, "Follow the Prophet," *Ensign* or *Liahona*, May 2014, 40.

11

Make Daring Promises

Truth has been restored to the earth. The most important truths in time and eternity are not hidden from view. They are given to us in plain and precious power. They are revealed in such a way that a little child can sense their validity. These truths are spoken to our souls. They are impressed upon our spirits. They are made manifest to us in ways that are comforting, consoling, and impressive.

Through my time on earth, I have come to sense with clarity how remarkable, distinctive, and special the restored gospel of Jesus Christ is. In this day and age where there is much said and written about Joseph Smith and other presidents of the Church, as well as about The Church of Jesus Christ of Latter-day Saints, it is important to sift truth from error (see Joseph Smith—History 1). Joseph gives us a reliable pattern of how we may come to know divine truth—we must listen to those who have already found the truth and then seek from the divine fountainhead directly for ourselves.

It is vital for each one of us to know the source of truth—God the Father and His Son Jesus Christ. We come to know through hearing the testimony of those who already know. We come to know through diligent study, fervent prayer, and sincere asking. We come to know by learning the doctrine, trying to keep the commandments, attending to our commitments and covenants, and pressing forward in a desire to believe. It is important to remember that this is a new gospel dispensation, a new commission. The heavens have been opened, priesthood has been conferred, keys have been bestowed, doctrine has been revealed, and ordinances have been made known. There have been prophets called, covenants made possible, spiritual gifts given, and directions received (see Doctrine and Covenants 1; 20).

As this is the most important quest of our lives, it is needful that we are aware of the potential pitfalls. We are wise to be wary of traps, obstacles, counterfeits, and deceptions. There are countless enticements along the way—everything from temptations to false doctrine to attacks on faith to distractions. This restored truth is the object of denigration, insult, misunderstanding, misrepresentation, and mockery. This should not surprise us. It has been that way since the beginning. Truth has always been under assault from the camps of both unbelieving hedonism and religious tradition. As we remember that restored truth always flies in the face of that which is pleasure seeking, popular, and transitory, we will have the fortitude to persist on the covenant path toward the destiny promised by modern-day prophets and the God who called them (see Doctrine and Covenants 76:1–10).

In this context, I note that the Lord has not called us to a life of comfort. Rather, He has invited us into the fellowship of His faith, the path of His designing, and the work of His heart. He beckons us to follow Him on the high road to triumph. Let us now examine three offerings we promise to make to God that will require much of us. These are the call to service, the invitation to evidence courage, and the need to show forth love.

The Promise to Serve

The opportunity to serve others is an honor. To give of ourselves in blessing someone else is a triumphant victory over the selfishness of our mortal flesh. To rise above self-interest and labor on behalf of another is a divine undertaking when approached in a spirit of helpfulness. It is rarely, if ever, easy or convenient to serve others. Service stretches the soul of the servant.

King Benjamin gave a great sermon on service that we can glean much rich insight from. Consider some of lessons he teaches us about godly leadership and service.

- Godly words are both spoken and written that we might unite in righteous causes (see Mosiah 2:9).
- Those called of God to lead conduct their ministry with the desire to share God's words. They do this so that the hearers may listen carefully with the intent to receive the word, act in accordance with true teaching, be touched in their hearts, and have greater understanding of God's secrets (see Mosiah 2:9).
- Godly leaders are not interested in having people fear them, praise them, or put them on spiritual pedestals (see Mosiah 2:10).
- Godly leaders are aware of their human limitations. They are also aware of their divine call and the great power of God in sustaining and preserving them. They know that they are in the hands of the Lord. They sense that they are called to devote themselves to the work with no reservation. They serve with a godly loyalty (see Mosiah 2:11).
- Leaders called of God are empowered and safeguarded by God. Their ministry is one of devoted service, not of using their people to get gain (see Mosiah 2:12).
- Spiritual leaders treat their people in accordance with the commandments of God. They promote righteousness in human relationships. They teach obedience to God so that men and women can know the blessings of how God interacts with us (see Mosiah 2:13).
- Righteous leaders work hard to serve their people and to treat them with dignity, honor, and respect. They regard them justly and fairly. The people thus served can see that their leaders are living in transparently good ways. The same laws and standards apply to leaders and the people (see Mosiah 2:14).

- Holy leaders are not boastful or self-seeking. They are not interested in castigating their people or in promoting their own elevation. They seek to live in such a way that God is pleased with them (see Mosiah 2:15).
- Good leaders serve God, always keeping in mind that He is their benefactor and guide. They use their lives for service (see Mosiah 2:16).
- God's leaders want people to know that true wisdom is to be found only in serving God by serving others. They serve a noble cause, a greater good than just serving their own interests (see Mosiah 2:17).
- Holy kings work to serve their subjects. Hence, it is right for citizens of God's kingdom to serve other citizens (see Mosiah 2:18).
- If it is right to thank mortal men for their faithful service, then it is so much more important to thank God for His everlasting righteous leadership (see Mosiah 2:19).
- Even if we give every possible expression of thanks, praise, and worship that is optimally possible for us to give to God—such as showing gratitude to God for creating us, giving us life, giving us agency, protecting us, blessing us with joy, and granting us societal peace—we would still find that we are eternally indebted to Him. God has given us more than we could ever give to Him (see Mosiah 2:20–21). Giving service to Him with everything we have and are makes sense to those whose whole souls swell with understanding of the great kindness, generosity, and mercy of God.

I periodically reflect on this great discourse. I am always reminded that God is good. I have not always sensed His great love and His profound blessings. To think on God more deliberately, deeply, and regularly is to be moved and reminded that He is better than we give Him credit for. I have not served God with my whole soul throughout my life, though there are certainly times when I have done so. It is a source of awe to me that God serves me with due diligence. He is anxiously engaged in serving me. He is showing me that He is invested in my life. This awareness inspires me to be better at appreciating Him and others around me. I think pondering on what God and His servants do for us can motivate us to serve in more holy ways. Indeed, we are reminded, "For how knoweth a man the master whom he has not served, and who is a stranger unto him, and is far from the thoughts and intents of his heart?" (Mosiah 5:13). If we think on God daily and feel His love as manifest through His constant efforts, then we are changed by that reflective consideration. We come to see God as involved in our lives. We become much more thoughtful, appreciative, and humble. We become more willing to serve.

God wants us to serve Him. He has invited us to:

- "Serve him with all diligence of mind" (Mosiah 7:33).
- Serve, love, and hold to God" (3 Nephi 13:24).
- "Serve the true and living God" (Mormon 9:28).
- "Worship God, for him only shalt thou serve" (Moses 1:15).
- "Choose ye this day, to serve the Lord God who made you" (Moses 6:33).
- Have a determination to serve God to the end (see Doctrine and Covenants 20:37).
- Devote all our service in Zion (see Doctrine and Covenants 24:7).
- Love God, serve Him, and keep all His commandments (see Doctrine and Covenants 42:29).
- "Love the Lord thy God . . . and in the name of Jesus Christ thou shalt serve him" (Doctrine and Covenants 59:5).

It is difficult to see how God could be any clearer with us. The command to serve Him is one that abounds with great love and rich promise. It is an invitation to a life of high adventure. Such a life is its own reward. Indeed, the Lord tells us, "I, the Lord, am merciful and gracious unto those who fear me, and delight to honor those who serve me in righteousness and in truth unto the end" (Doctrine and Covenants 76:5). While a life of service may not seem very appealing, it is a life of great fulfillment. It is an education into the ways of the

Almighty. It gives us an insider view to how God spends His time and on what causes He directs His energies. Embodied in the service we offer to God is the service we render to His children. To serve a soul is to bless a soul.

God is gathering souls to Him in these last days. Indeed, God is the great gatherer. This is the long-promised day when hunters and fishers would be commissioned anew to gather those who are scattered. The family of God is not to remain eternally fractured. Rather, the sheep that are lost are to be found. Our Father and His Son, Jesus Christ, have opened the heavens in our day through Joseph Smith so that the knowledge and authority to gather scattered Israel can be received. This gathering represents the effort of all efforts. It is the outpouring of God's redemptive power throughout all the world—His vineyard. God's love is drawing all who will hear to come to the covenants of salvation and exaltation. This holy unity is our great work.

I was thrilled in the April 2022 general conference to hear the President of the Church, two Apostles, and a Seventy repeat the divine charge for young men to serve a mission for the Lord, for sisters who desire to do so, and for couples to prepare where possible. My mission changed my life. My mission president taught me about priesthood power, pure revealed doctrine, and how to obtain confidence in the presence of God. My companions taught me brotherly love in a way I had never known before and can never forget. The sisters I served with had great enthusiasm in the work of the Lord. The couples I knew brought wisdom and maturity to the work.

I was grateful as a missionary to be taught by Elder M. Russell Ballard and Elder Jeffrey R. Holland in person on several occasions. I was tremendously grateful for so many members I worked with in Birmingham, England, and their profound impact for good on me. I was blessed to teach some fine people and see them progress to the waters of baptism and to the temple. I came to love Joseph Smith and Jesus Christ with profound depth as a young missionary. How thankful I am for the opportunity I had thirty-two years ago for my call to serve. I was far from perfect, but the Lord was merciful and kind to me in my immaturity and inexperience. He has brought me along and allowed me to learn of Him. I join my voice in saying that serving a mission is a marvelous blessing. It was extremely difficult and simultaneously wonderfully rewarding. I hope all young men will heed the prophetic call. They will not regret it!

Our offering of the restored gospel to our children and others is the greatest act of service we could ever perform. We are inviting souls to come to the covenants of salvation and exaltation. We are seeking to rescue others from sin and death. I think of the message of rescuing through the gospel covenant, and that makes a substantial difference in how I see sharing of the word—it makes a difference to my understanding, power, and spirit. We are, of course, seeking to rescue refugees from cold, war, famine, and so on. However, we also want to rescue them from the greater enemies of sin and death. We are seeking to save souls in every sense possible. We should never lose sight of that supreme goal, although obviously we can serve others without them ever accepting the invitation to be exalted. The gospel involves more than temporal or social benevolence—it includes revelation of the laws, commandments, ordinances, covenants, attributes, and powers necessary for each one of us to rise to eternal perfection. The deep truths are hidden from all those not yet ready to see them. The whole gospel is essential. I am grateful that God gives us eyes to see and ears to hear when we are ready and willing!

For example:

- To clothe the naked is to give them physical clothing, but it can also mean to give temple clothing to the spiritually unclothed.
- To feed the hungry can refer to both physical food and spiritual nourishment. Truly, sacrament bread is the food for the spiritually malnourished.
- To give drink to the thirsty can mean both water and the truths of salvation. Indeed, the sacrament water is a quenching of the thirst of the spiritually thirsty.
- To heal the sick can relate both to temporal support and spiritual blessings such as priesthood administrations.

- To give shelter to the homeless is both to house them in temporal abodes and to give them a place in God's kingdom.

Let us not only give of our temporal substance but also offer spiritual renewal and refreshment through the spiritual feast available only in the household of faith. Of course, we can administer resources to the tired, lonely, blind, deaf, and cast out. We can also give our unique spiritual resources to bring souls to the table of Jehovah, to the wedding feast of the Lamb, to the mountain of the Lord, and to the everlasting kingdom of our God.

The Promise of Bravery

I have come to believe that to become perfect in Christ, we must be made perfect in each Christlike attribute. One of these characteristics is bravery—the willingness to show courage when it is evidently difficult to do so. I honor, respect, and admire true prophets of God. They possess and evidence "courage under fire," especially when it is difficult to do so. We are blessed to have prophets who speak the truth in love to us, particularly when it means they are confronting us to change our ways! For example, the prophet Jeremiah was ready to do difficult things for God. His love and spiritual conviction were such that he continually preached repentance to ancient Israel—even though he was rejected for doing so. He declared that God would gather scattered Israel in the latter days, that the promises of God will stand, that the loving kindness of God's covenant will stand the test of time, that the Messiah will reign in the latter days, and that the covenant people of the Lord will flourish in the abundance, comfort, knowledge, and joy of the Lord. This was and is a message of mercy, hope, thanksgiving, and redemption for all the world. As we repent and come to God, we can know His bounteous blessings.

One of the ways we show bravery in defending the cause of the Lord is by showing loyalty to those He sends in His name. We need to be very discerning in these last days. For example, efforts abound to diminish the name, role, character, and testimony of the Prophet Joseph Smith. We ought not to fall prey to this devious trap of our enemy. When Moroni said to Joseph that his name would be had for both good and evil among all nations, kindreds, tongues, and people, it is evident that this prophecy would even apply to those inside the Church. I have found that those who are loyal to Joseph's special call are sustained by the Lord in very significant ways. Joseph was—and is—a prophet's Prophet. We can come to comprehend the greatness of the Restoration that came through him. It is an astonishing work. The spirit of prophecy and revelation attends those who come to know for themselves that Joseph is the choice seer—the *Messiah ben Joseph* prophesied of. I hope we will share this message in clear and undiluted ways. Our salvation depends upon us receiving the word through Joseph because this is how we demonstrate that we receive Christ in our day. The people in the time of Moses could not accept Jehovah while denouncing Moses. To accept the messenger is to accept the Master who sent Him. I love Joseph, and I love the Lord who commissioned him!

As prophets need to show bravery, tenacity, and spiritual resilience, so do all of us who wish to engage in the errand of the Lord. We need to have courage in accepting, acting upon, and defending the cause of prophets. Whom God has commissioned, let not man reject. I have that feeling about Joseph Smith. The revelations declare that His name would be had for good and evil among all nations, kindreds, tongues, and people. That has definitely come to pass. To some, Joseph is a fraud or a fallen prophet. To me, he is a true prophet. I believe and know that he was called of God. I accept his teachings as being the mind, will, voice, and word of God and the power of God unto salvation. I am a witness that his First Vision was the beginning of many great and glorious revelations. I have tasted the holy fruit that has come to me and my loved ones through the great latter-day work Joseph was appointed to restore. Our safety lies in having a Spirit-revealed witness that Joseph was on the Lord's errand. There is tremendous safety, comfort, fortitude, and anchoring in this testimony. I honor our dear brother Joseph.

This is a message worth pondering over, a cause worth carefully considering. It is an idea to reflect upon in our day of division and consternation. God invites us to think about, feel toward, and act on His directives. By this means we are called to stand for something difficult, to raise our voice in sustaining a unique mission. Let us not be afraid of the world or of our distinctive doctrine. Let us not be ashamed of our unique claims to a fullness of truth and a bestowal of divine authority. Our God-assisted efforts to curb our tempers, control our tongues, and maintain our composure under hostile situations will bless us, our families, our friends, our neighbors, our enemies, and all the world.

I have pondered on those Saints of ancient and latter days who showed the courage of true conviction. Their example encourages me to know that I can do hard things for the Lord when needed. When we know we have truth on our side and when we are disposed by a spirit of true love, we can do things that move others in great ways. Our desire for goodness will sometimes be opposed. Our seeking after righteousness must be tested. It is wise to expect that opposition will confront us. As we aim to receive inspiration and make great plans, it is vital to note that it will not always be easy. However, as we trust in God, show determination, and move forward, we will accomplish marvelous things in our lives. God wants us to do good, and He will help us. As we are resisted, we can increase our efforts and gain the victory. It is my view that the greater the opposition against us, the more important it is that we go forward in faith. We need something of great spiritual fire within us. This fire of truth and testimony can help us to face extraordinary difficulties and surmount tremendous obstacles. We need a measure of passion for things divine if we are to persist in righteousness through treacherous dangers all around us. We can rise above! Then our example can light a powerful fire in others.

It is evident that courage is one of the requirements that a disciple needs to enter the celestial heaven. Indeed, those who inherit the terrestrial kingdom "are not valiant in the testimony of Jesus; wherefore, they obtain not the crown over the kingdom of our God" (Doctrine and Covenants 76:79). Although they have the testimony of Jesus, they are not valiant in it. They do not evidence the necessary valor when it comes to standing up for Christ and His cause. A valiant person is willing to put their reputation on the line. They know that standing up for Christ and His great latter-day work is fraught with the potential for trouble, but they do it anyway. Like a firefighter who enters a burning building to save a child, they show they are willing to suffer negative consequences for the Lord. The obtaining of a crown requires uncommon courage and resilience. Those who are not brave in the cause of Christ cannot fully overcome the world. Hence, they cannot be rewarded with the same victorious blessings in God's kingdom that the fearless of heart can be.

Christ is hated by some and ignored by many. This is the reason Christ had to have valiant courage in the Father's cause when He walked the earth. He was opposed and rejected—even by some of His own people—and it would have been easy to throw in the towel, to give up, to relinquish the heavy demands. His perfect love was fearless (see 1 John 4:18). This was not the absence of fear but the willingness to overcome fear with bravery. In His cause, we are to have the courage to change, care, and correct others when needed. We are to have the bravery to show our faith in public, to testify to unpopular truths, to try to resemble our Lord.

Hence, we are given the following examples of godly courage:

- The sons of Mosiah "took courage to go forth unto the Lamanites to declare unto them the word of God" (Alma 17:12).
- The sons of the Lamanites converted by Ammon were "exceedingly valiant for courage" (Alma 53: 20). Captain Helaman, in speaking of the attributes of these young men, said to Moroni that "never had I seen so great courage, nay, not amongst all the Nephites" (Alma 56:45). Even when outnumbered, they said, "We did take courage with our small force which we had received, and were fixed with a determination to conquer our enemies, and to maintain our lands, and our possessions, and our wives, and our children, and the cause of our liberty" (Alma 58:12).

- When Captain Moroni was assured of the faithfulness of Pahoran against great odds, we are told that "his heart did take courage" (Alma 62:10).
- The warring Lamanites knew that the Nephites had "exceedingly great courage" (Alma 62:19).
- When Nephi and Lehi were under siege from antagonistic enemies, they were encircled by fire. It is reported that "when they saw that they were encircled about with a pillar of fire, and that it burned them not, their hearts did take courage" (Helaman 5:23–24).
- Moroni, in speaking the correcting words of God, said, "Behold, I speak with boldness, having authority from God; and I fear not what man can do; for perfect love casteth out all fear" (Moroni 8:16).
- The Prophet Joseph Smith, when facing dire persecution from relentless enemies (including betrayal from once loyal friends), shared this message with the beleaguered saints: "Brethren, shall we not go on in so great a cause? Go forward and not backward. Courage, brethren; and on, on to the victory!" (Doctrine and Covenants 128:22).

All these examples occurred within the context of great tribulation. These Saints showed their resolve by sticking with the message or errand given to them by God. As we cultivate such courage, we can do likewise. We will then inspire others to ignite the courage of God in their own lives.

I know I have sometimes found it hard to be a practicing Latter-day Saint when so many cultural values clash ostensibly and aggressively with the standards of the gospel. I was scared to try to engineer discussions in positive directions or influence people in righteous ways. I was either worried about the consequences or lacked faith in people. But there were times I stood up for my beliefs, and I found that to be very satisfying, even if they did not respond with great positivity.

I remember one act of spiritual courage in my own life that was a significant and defining moment for me. It was a moment that is etched in my memory. This experience was when I worked in a service station as a seventeen-year-old youth. A fellow worker picked up money from the ground that two customers had inadvertently dropped. I saw this happen. The customers came back and asked if anyone had found the money. The worker denied seeing it. He even tried to lay the blame on my brother, who was also working there at the time. I was frustrated and approached them all. I said I knew he had the money and that he better admit to it. It was a brave move (some would even say "foolish"), but I felt the fire of truth within me, and I would not yield. Rarely in my life have I felt the Spirit so strongly as at that moment. He gave back the money. I thought my fellow worker would hate me for what I did, but he did not. I even got to share with him about the Articles of Faith of our Church. I sensed that he respected me for standing up for my principles. I later bore testimony of this event at an Ireland youth conference and felt that same fire of faith indicating that honesty and courage are pleasing to God.

The Promise to Give Encouraging Love

When we have been encouraged by the gospel message, it is anticipated that we will go forth to encourage others. Our message to the world is the most sublime that can exist. It is the truth that encourages men and women to the highest possible extent. It is the vantage point of God, the message of the ages, the word that inspires people in marvelous ways. Let us fulfill our role of counseling others according to God's perspective. Our glorious doctrine, our listening ear, our warm friendship, our sound advice, our Spirit-led invitations—these things will enable us to uplift, edify and empower the people of the world in the most divine ways possible. We are privileged to share this motivating truth with the world.

Christ can replace enmity with kindness, return friendship for hostility, overcome animosity with tenderness, banish resentment and instead cultivate forgiveness. He can transform our contempt and give us regard for others. He can help us to transcend hatred and foster true and deep love. He wants us to develop these attributes within our souls so that we might help others find the same transformative newness we have found. Christ saves both obedient Saint and repentant sinner. As Christ can change us, so we can be agents tasked with the desire and gifts to help others find change in Christ.

Our charge to show love often occurs in the context of inconvenience. We meet the lonely, scared, despairing, burdened, and hurt. Our efforts can strengthen them greatly. Our words to them do matter, our actions have a healing impact, and our prayers bless their lives. By stretching ourselves, we gain their trust and affection. There are those around us who sometimes are starved for a word of appreciation, for a moment of genuine attention, for a listening ear, for a guiding hand, for an expression of confidence, for a gentle gesture, for a mention of praise, for a loving hug, for a sincere smile. There are those who are downtrodden, fearful, alone, saddened, and dejected. Our voice can be raised in encouragement. Our expressions can be ones of concern. We can show interest in them, appreciate their strivings, notice their accomplishments, and commend their efforts.

Did the tired, hungry, and somewhat despondent Alma appreciate the food, shelter, and listening ear of Amulek (see Alma 8:21–27)? Of course! Did Joseph Smith appreciate the sweet companionship of Hyrum Smith, Willard Richards, and John Taylor in Carthage Jail (see Doctrine and Covenants 135)? Indeed! Showing love, empathy, and encouragement to others provides a balm of hopeful healing in all times and seasons, especially painful ones.

I hope we remember that difficult circumstances are often the seedbed for profound experiences. The tribulations of mortality can be used to spiritual advantage in our personal lives, our families, the Church, and indeed the entire earth. I hope others will see the hand of God in their lives in a way that will edify them and give them renewed hope. In every challenge we face, we can draw closer to God and learn how to effectively inspire others to draw close to the source of their salvation. Surely God is greatly pleased when we represent Him in bountiful ways to His other children. Service, bravery, and love are gifts of deep and eternal import.

12
Have Lofty Expectations

Our Lord has high expectations of us, sometimes asking us to do very hard things. The doing of these challenging things is an essential part of the process of perfection. I view His obligations as a sign of His trust and confidence in us. He wants us to live nobly, to take the high road, to take up our crosses, to reach for the best we are capable of. I am inspired by His vision of us. I believe each of us can come to know that whatever God asks of us can be achieved. We can do great and amazing things in and through God.

The three lofty anticipations, in my mind, are forgiveness, righteous judgment, and empathy. Before we can truly forgive others, we must come to know forgiveness ourselves. Before we can judge others righteously, we must first be judged righteously ourselves. Before we can develop and show real empathy for others, we must have empathy shown to us first. It is my experience that in and through Christ, we can know these three great gifts. Then we will be positioned to offer them to others.

Forgiven in Christ

The gospel of Christ invites us to be baptized unto repentance and to be washed from our sins through Him who is "mighty to save and to cleanse from all unrighteousness" (Alma 7:14). No sins could be forgiven were it not for Him. No redemption from iniquity would be possible without His sacrifice. It is only when we come to sense His loving forgiveness that we truly feel the bounteous gift that such merciful reclamation offers to us. Our Savior is a loving Lord. He is stronger than we sometimes think. He is a remarkable Redeemer who snatches us from death, hell, the devil, sin, and every kind and type of self-destructive behavior. His mercy is touching. He has gone the ultimate distance to rescue us from our own weaknesses, from the clutches of the world, and from the grasp of addictive chains. His great power is to save.

Forgive Others

To forgive is no easy task. That is why it brings such great rewards with it. It is a noble pursuit, a generous endeavor. It is beyond natural impulses. It is so soothing and magnanimously healing to us and others to do it. To forgive another is to reach not only for the best in *them*—it is also to see the best within our *own* souls. It is to truly love yourself, set yourself free, believe in yourself, and allow yourself to be beautiful. Forgiveness is a miraculous mercy. Do yourself a favor and forgive everyone everything. There is no better way of treating yourself respectfully than this. It is a wonderful gift to extend to another. The Savior is pleased when we offer others forgiveness.

Judged Righteously in Christ

We are given a fair and compassionate hearing by the Son of God. He has chastened me in direct and gentle ways when I have needed it. He has encouraged me to come to Him. When I have sought forgiveness from my Father in Heaven and people I have wounded, I have found response. I have discovered the forgiveness I have sought. I have felt that the Savior calls me to repentance for my misdeeds. He has not concealed His thoughts. He has indicated His disappointment. He has asked me to stop doing wrong and to start doing right. He has asked me to do more good things and less bad things. He has expected me to learn, grow, and improve. He has also encouraged me, supported me, and sustained me. I feel understood by Him and rightly judged. I feel He knows exactly who I am and asks me to be what I need to be. I have never felt falsely accused by Him or misjudged. He knows my shortcomings and plainly indicates what course I should follow. His messaging is consistent. His standards don't change.

Righteous Judgment of Others

Viewpoints about judgment abound. Few topics generate as much conflict as this one. I hope I can offer a unique contribution to this important subject. Consider the words of our Lord:

> And now it came to pass that when Jesus had spoken these words he turned again to the multitude, and did open his mouth unto them again, saying: Verily, verily, I say unto you, Judge not, that ye be not judged.
> For with what judgment ye judge, ye shall be judged; and with what measure ye mete, it shall be measured to you again.
> And why beholdest thou the mote that is in thy brother's eye, but considerest not the beam that is in thine own eye?
> Or how wilt thou say to thy brother: Let me pull the mote out of thine eye—and behold, a beam is in thine own eye?
> Thou hypocrite, first cast the beam out of thine own eye; and then shalt thou see clearly to cast the mote out of thy brother's eye. (3 Nephi 14:1–5)

Let us take a moment to ponder this doctrine. Was He saying, "Do not ever make any judgments about anything"? I do not believe so. He was warning the people of Nephi—a people who had seen their friends and family members destroyed due to gross iniquity. These were good people who needed to be reminded to keep themselves in the right way and to stay on the correct path. He was teaching them that judgment needs to be done in the right way. He was instructing them to avoid a kind of judgment that boomerangs back against them, a type of self-righteous judgment that sees wrong only in others but not in oneself. This kind of judgment is the kind that actually condemns both the person making the judgment and the person being judged. It is the judgment of the Pharisees. The Pharisees judged others harshly and by so doing cut themselves off from being judged in anything other than harsh ways. Their judgment was like a sword that cut into the people they judged and maimed them at the same time.

Christ does not judge in this unfair and unrighteous fashion. He judges us according to what is right and good. He judges us according to standards we can live and values we can possess. He was saying to the people that they should judge only in situations where their own shortcomings were clear to them and subsequently removed by them. Then, and only then, could they see clearly to assist others in overcoming their much smaller faults and failings. He was saying to those who desired to be righteous to look inward and rectify their own lives first. Then they could appropriately judge or discern or see where others were lacking and help them to find relief from errors and sinful burdens. This is a message about learning how to judge as Christ does, not about making no value judgments at all.

I think that judgment is often incorrectly construed in a negative sense. The connotation is one of criticism, unfairness, and harshness. Many seem to think that any practice of judgment is inherently lacking compassion, understanding, sympathy, and empathy. This is an incomplete assessment. Let us reflect on some of the scriptural and pragmatic incidences of judgment.

Here are some examples of judgment in the scriptures:

- King Solomon judging between two women, each of whom claimed to be mother to the same child
- Christ not condemning the woman taken in adultery
- Christ cleansing the temple
- Christ not talking to Herod

These judgments show that Christ did not agree with certain types of behavior. He taught both obedience and repentance. He advocated both justice and mercy. Likewise, so did prophets and kings.

The following are examples of judgment in the Church from a bishop or other leader:

- Restriction of opportunities to partake of the sacrament or other ordinances
- Restriction of privileges to speak, teach, pray, or otherwise serve at church
- Withdrawal of Church membership

These various restrictions are not intended to indicate that persons are worthless or useless. They make a judgment based on behavior, not on the worth of someone's soul. They attach a consequence to an action that is deemed to be out of alignment with Church doctrine.

Finally, there are also examples of judgment in a court of law:

- Financial penalties
- Sentences of incarceration
- Withdrawal of driving licenses

These judgments are penalties for behavior that is illegal and/or dangerous. Without the possibility of such outcomes, crime would effectively be seen as acceptable and even appropriate behavior. Legal judgments can be concerned with both "private" and "public" actions. In this sense, they incorporate both the individual and their relationships. Judgment weighs up the relevant factors such as age and maturity of person, the status of the person (obviously those holding high status are more visible and therefore more subject to scrutiny by everyone), the nature of the behavior, whether the behavior is a singular incident or a pattern, the impact of the behavior on others (especially the innocent), whether the behavior is in the public domain, and the degree of contrition of the person.

Prudential judgment focuses on the behavior of the person. It is not an assessment of all aspects of a person's life or their nature or worth. It is an examination of their actions in the context of their beliefs and position in society. Wise and careful judgment is essential to any properly functioning society, including religious societies. Wise judges need to consider all relevant factors, to the extent they are known, and weigh them up in a judicious manner to arrive at an appropriate decision. For example, admission of a sin or crime after being caught cannot be seen in the same light as voluntary confession prior to being caught. Humble recognition of wrongdoing is far better than admission or denial after being implicated. One suggests willingness to accept personal responsibility while the other does not. Reason demands that genuine contrition be treated more leniently than reckless abandon or defiance.

Judgment starts from the foundation that some behaviors are acceptable while others are not. Consequently, each of the Ten Commandments reflects a moral position on certain actions:

- *Thou shalt not kill*—We have no right to take the mortal lives of other persons away. God gave them life, and we should honor and respect that gift.
- *Thou shalt not steal*—Taking away the belongings of others is not approved of by God.
- *Thou shalt not commit adultery*—Marriage is important in God's plan, and the protections and limitations incorporated into it safeguard its sanctity.
- *Thou shalt not bear false witness*—God does not want us spreading mistruths about situations or other people. He loves the truth!
- *Thou shalt not covet*—God does not want us desiring the belongings or status of others, as such selfish wants may also lead to behavior that is violent or criminal.
- *Thou shalt not take the name of the Lord thy God in vain*—God wants us to use His name respectfully, reverently, and only with authority. Blasphemy is not a moral virtue.
- *Thou shalt have no other gods before me*—God wants our relationship with Him to be the first great priority of our lives.
- *Thou shalt not make unto thee any graven image*—The worship of false gods in any form takes us away from the true and living God, yielding disastrous consequences for us.

- *Honor thy father and mother*—God cares about our showing deference, respect, honor, and admiration to our earthly parents.
- *Keep the Sabbath day holy*—God cares that we set time aside for weekly worship, remembrance, and pondering on Him and His sacred plans and places.

Judgment is a relevant factor in life for all sorts of activities. We don't trust pilots, doctors, lawyers, or electricians who cheated on their examinations. Without sufficient training, expertise, and reliability, every function in society would be essentially impossible. Obviously, there is a difference between technical acumen and moral conscientious. However, they are both important. A financial investor might be very skilled when investing our money, but if they are also morally corrupt, they might easily steal the funds they invested on our behalf. Hence, it is not enough to be competent or skillful in a role—one also needs to be morally honest and upright so that trust can be placed in the person responsible for seeing that the role is performed correctly. Otherwise, society would collapse.

The idea that we should make righteous judgments parallels what God and His prophets do. These judgments are not intended to be rash, haphazard, ill-founded, or partial. Rather, they are to reflect an understanding of life that accepts there is a difference between right and wrong at a fundamental level. Even in situations where people do not accept the authority of a Judeo-Christian framework, they must accept some standards as being desirable while others are not. Humans can't live without making judgments. Life would be impossible without it. Even those who do not believe in God would not be happy to live in a world where their goods could be stolen, their good names reviled without cause, and their relationships breached at will by others. There must be some standards in life. There must be codes of conduct. Otherwise, we could not know how to live, how to form bonds with others, or what to expect from institutions around us.

Some tell others not to make any judgments at all. What they mean is that their views should never be held up to any sort of critical examination. I confess that this opinion has never made any sense to me. This is akin to saying, "You can think or say only what I allow you to think or say." It is an impossible expectation. What most people really mean when they say "Don't judge me" is "Don't weigh my choices according to your criteria—only examine them relating to mine." This is one-sided. It is an unworkable method to adopt. All viewpoints, attitudes, actions, and lifestyles must be subject to serious examination if we are to consider adopting them as codes of belief and conduct. Moral judgments are built into the very fabric of what it means to be human. God has made it so.

From a pragmatic viewpoint, we all must make judgments about the food we like, the music we love, the clothing that inspires us, and the places we love to visit. By implication, these judgments only make sense when contrasted against other alternatives. I do not see how it is possible to like all types of food, love all types of music, value all expressions of art, and so on. Inevitably there will be music we love and music we hate. Even when it comes to other people, it is seemingly impossible for us to like or appreciate everyone we meet. We tend to prefer some people to others. We also tend to trust some people and not others. This form of judgment may sometimes be appropriate.

At the ideological level, there will always be values and beliefs we align with and others that are repugnant to us. We must make sense of the options available to us by comparing different viewpoints. These are not just abstract decisions. They are located within a value system. To feel strongly about the value of life is to simultaneously hold strong views about murder!

It also ought to be observed that judgment can be positive and beneficial. If I fail my driving test due to not taking sufficient care regarding the use of my mirrors, a failing grade should point me to the fact that I need to remedy my error. If I accept this correction, then I will in due course pass my test. More importantly, I will be a safer driver—hopefully! Judgment in this case is in truth a blessing. It is a safety and defense against incautious behavior. This could save lives. We far too often assume that all judgment is inherently negative and critical (as in criticism or a harsh view of something). This is a perception that fails to take account of the reason behind the judgment, which is to ensure that people are properly prepared to receive the privileges they are seeking.

Judgment does not necessarily inherently lack mercy or compassion. We can hold feelings of sympathy or empathy for a person who fails an exam while simultaneously being aware that they should have studied more diligently in preparation. These are not mutually exclusive positions to hold. Mothers, for example, often remind their children to clean their rooms or eat their vegetables or do their homework. This does not mean the mother does not love her children. While children usually do not appreciate the reminders and may resist the directive, they will generally in time come to see that the dictate was an evidence of parental love rather than proof that it was lacking. In other words, parental judgment about the limitations in acceptable performance of a child should not be automatically construed as unrighteous judgment or dominion.

Is there such a thing as unrighteous judgment? Of course there is. Some judgments are biased, self-serving, incorrect, or otherwise dubious. Judgments may be incomplete or inaccurate. However, this does not mean that any judgment is automatically wrong, although it must be open to reasonable scrutiny. It is important that judgments be well-founded and fair. This is not an easy task, and all of us fall short from time to time. I do believe that as we mature, we learn to make wiser judgments.

Surely Christ did not mean never make judgments at all. This cannot be a proper reading of what He said or meant. What is actually written is "judge not, that ye be not judged" (Matthew 7:1) and "judge righteous judgment" (John 7:24). The inspired version renders it this way—"Judge not *unrighteously*, that ye be not judged: *but judge righteous judgment*" (Joseph Smith Translation, Matthew 7:2 [Matthew 7:1, footnote *a*]; emphasis added). He clearly did not mean to infer the idea that we should accept all beliefs as equally valid or all viewpoints as being morally equivalent or all actions as being good. Such a view contradicts His teachings that we need to accept Him to be saved. Accepting Him as our Savior is a value judgment. The very notion implies that we are simultaneously rejecting all other potential saviors, and we are also rejecting the idea of there being no Savior whatsoever. Hence, He said, "You cannot serve God and mammon" (Matthew 6:24). Obviously, this is a judgment because it endorses the idea that we should serve God and simultaneously encourages people not to serve worldliness. It is to prefer one way of living over another. It is to indicate that we cannot pursue two moral opposites at the same time.

What Christ meant to convey was to not judge others unless you yourself wish to be likewise judged. In other words, be fair and just in your judgments. Only apply judgments that could be used on you—the Golden Rule, if you like. Also, make judgments that are righteous, meaning based on true and righteous principles. This does not imply a rejection of divine law or a refusal of moral standards. Instead, it locates all judgments within the framework that some principles are good and true while some are not.

As we come to think more as Christ does, we will see that our judgments are far better. This means improved judgments, not the absence of judgments. For example:

- If Christ came to earth today, in His resurrected form, would He say that all viewpoints are equally valid? No.
- Would He say that love takes preference over law so that to love someone means endorsing and celebrating every position they advocate? Of course not.
- Would He say that we must wholeheartedly accept any opinion that contradicts the commandments of God to show alignment with others in Christlike ways? No, certainly not.

I do not feel duty-bound to believe everything I once believed. I have learned to discriminate between good and bad. Nor do I feel obligated to accept every viewpoint held by the people around me, even if they are believers in God. I don't think I have to agree with someone to love them. I hold myself responsible to ask myself what the opinion of God is and then hold to that. I am concerned about the view of God on every matter. I want to believe what He believes, to love what He loves, to safeguard what He values.

Of course, I do not endeavor to force anyone to agree with me, but I do think it is acceptable to use persuasion to display the coherence of logically consistent divine perspectives. In this way, others will be able to see the merit of God's truth. The commandments of God make so much sense to me. Most of us would not want to live in a world where the commandments were breached most of the time. Such a world would involve constant danger and chaos.

We can learn to judge in Christlike ways. We see the truth of a situation and judge accordingly. We distinguish good from harmful. We differentiate right from wrong. We discern between friend and foe. We know when we are being told the truth and when we are being lied to. We detect the gospel of Christ as being different from the doctrines of devils or the commandments of men. Christ was aware. He was not blind to the realities of the world. He saw right through people. He knew if they were deceivers or not, if they were pure or not, if they were believers or not. There are wolves in sheep's clothing. There are ravenous wolves in the world. Christ has enemies, just like He has friends.

We need to know the difference between an idea that comes from God and one that originates with the enemy, between the holy and the profane, between the light of heaven and the darkness of hell. We can rely on what we feel and sense. If we are living righteously, we will be warned about who not to trust and what beliefs are dangerous. Let us be harmless as doves but also wise as serpents. Don't fall prey to the false idea that you must accept everything and anything you are told to be a good follower of Christ. You can love people and still disagree with their views, values, and actions. Christ Himself advocated love of all men but not the following of the ways of all men.

Receive Empathy from Christ

I hope you have had the experience of sensing that the Savior has seen you for something more than you are. I hope you have felt that He is kind to you, even when you are shortsighted, angry, selfish, or antagonistic. To come to know that He sees both your good traits and bad behaviors and also understands all the conditioning circumstances of your life is an important experience to have. He sees what you control and what controls you. He has a clearer and more long-term perspective of your worth and possibilities than you do. I do not feel immediately condemned by Christ even when I fall short of His standards. Rather, I feel strongly that He is patiently persisting with me that I might grow slowly and surely toward a better way of life. I am grateful to feel that He views me with a big-hearted love rather than being quick to cast me off. It is a remarkably powerful thing to know that Christ has empathy for me, even in my smallness of soul. He believes and hopes that there is more to me than my mistakes, sins, foolishness, and pride. In fact, He knows there is. I feel and know that truth.

Show Empathy to Others

Who are the downtrodden? Where are the lonely? What of those in spiritual poverty? Who are the frightened and the sad? Sometimes it is us. It is you. It is me. It is all of us. We are the ones feeling in need of comfort and consolation. The Son of God spoke to the afflicted in their sorrow (see 3 Nephi 11–12). He pronounced blessings upon them. These blessings were offered to the meek who were sometimes poor in spirit, sometimes persecuted, sometimes sick, sometimes disappointed, sometimes grieving. His blessings were both temporary comforts and eternal promises. His blessings of peace were given in a fallen world to those who had need for both healing in mortality and hope for heaven. Be assured that as we come unto Christ, we will always find a blessing in the here and now that will somehow help us to navigate this weary world. In due course, our joy will be full forever.

I believe we can learn to listen to others, to sense their need, to almost see inside their souls as it were. We can feel something of their trouble. We can feel sympathy, compassion, and even empathy for them. This is possible because as we come to Christ, He allows us to see the hidden need, the real longing, the genuine sorrows of others. As Christ consoles us with kindness, we learn how to become comforters of others (see Alma 26:27; 3 Nephi 17:21–22).

Can we receive comfort from the afflicted? Yes, of course. We can also receive love from those who are mourning, solace from those who are troubled, and companionship from those who are lonely. How? Well, those who are suffering are called to minister to others who are suffering. As they reach out in righteous love to console others, they both give comfort and receive it. Similarly, those who are reached out to are doubly blessed—as they give place to receive comfort, they also pay attention to the efforts of those ministering to them and they listen to them and serve them. In this process, both giver and receiver are consoled, edified, and instructed. This is the intelligent and comforting plan of the Lord.

13

SENSE PRIZED ANTICIPATIONS

I RETURN BRIEFLY TO THE STORY OF *A CHRISTMAS CAROL* BY CHARLES Dickens. I often think of the mythical character Ebenezer Scrooge, the central figure in the story. His story is a fascinating one. Scrooge is always focused on acquiring more money. He thinks in terms of what he wants to obtain rather than what good he can do with his life. In many ways, he has a short-sighted view. It is a narrow focus on a particular goal, a set outcome. He dwells on what is immediately pressing upon him—the desire for gain. However, he does not use his resources wisely. He hoards them with little or no benefit to himself or anyone else. He gets no light or heat from his money, no warmth from his possessions, no companionship from his coins, no joy from his ventures. He is so prudential as to be stingy. He lives as a loner. His life is a solitary one. Although he is financially secure, he does not get the possible benefits from his earnings that he could have.

Then—through the process of visiting the past, really seeing the present for the first time, and anticipating the possible dire consequences of his lifestyle—he finally begins to understand his life. He is introduced to the world of others in a new way. He acquires a change in perspective. He comes to see the past, present, and future in vivid ways as the ghosts show him his life, the ramifications of his choices, and the outcomes of his actions. He begins to acquire a long view. He changes from being selfish, shortsighted, and mean to being benevolent, kind, sharing, happy, rejoicing, and enjoyment-focused. He uses his resources to assist the poor and needy and to bring comfort and gladness to those within his sphere of influence. In this transformation, Scrooge retains his material riches and his ability to make money, but he also acquires the capacity to live a rich life in many other ways—in terms of relationships, viewpoints, and experiences. He comes to evaluate his life not just in material terms but also in qualitative senses. He comes to live life, not simply to be alive.

In like manner, our choices today lead to consequences in the future—sometimes a very long time away. The results of our actions are not obvious or quickly apparent to us, hence the danger of basing our choices on strong momentary desires alone. Doing so can obscure outcomes that are not desirable in the long run. So as we make decisions based on good principles now—although this might be a hard path and a difficult way now—this will benefit and bless others in the long run. Scrooge had to face some hard truths in the adventure he had with the guiding ghosts. These were not comfortable to him in the moment, but they ended up being advantageous in the long run as they helped him to craft the ability to see with a long-term perspective and a broad sense of understanding. The spirit of transformation that Scrooge experienced is the spirit of Christmas. It is the spirit of change, of renewal, of becoming wiser, of starting again, of living with a fresh viewpoint. The message is that we should not be either hedonistic or wasteful, but that we should use resources to enjoy life and use treasures to help people. We are to gain warmth from our friendships, joviality from our connections, and gratitude from our opportunities.

Some examples of taking the long view—especially in spiritual matters—can be seen in the holy scriptures:

- Adam and Eve were willing to face the lone and dreary world because they were able to foresee that a better one awaited after it.
- Noah built the ark for a rainy day because he knew it would save his people when the floods came.
- Lehi left Jerusalem, treasures, and prestige to encounter difficulties in the wilderness. Why? To find the promised land. Yes, they wandered for eight years in challenging circumstances, but they eventually found their way to a land flowing with abundance.
- The angels, shepherds, and wise men worshipped the Christ child long before He atoned for the sins of the world. Their difficult journey was amply rewarded with the hopeful anticipation of a far-off but inevitable victory.
- Jesus the Christ was willing to face the burdens of monumental affliction to obtain a glorious universal resurrection and a kingdom of glory for billions of His brothers and sisters.
- Joseph Smith viewed his deep persecution through the lens of knowledge that a latter-day Zion would eventually be founded.

All these examples contain the ability to see afar off to a better time. This perspective allowed these great souls to confront terrible problems in the moment with poise and confidence. The gospel perspective is not just a momentary one. It allows us to see into the past, present, and future. Our legacy is to face challenges now to enjoy benefits later. Some may see this as naive, foolish, or gullible. However, with the enhanced vantage point that the gospel offers, we can make decisions based on eternal implications. We are granted confidence that our path is heaven-blessed, even though it is uphill and demanding.

Those now choosing to not believe in God will not discern the outcomes of doing so until the future consequences arrive. Those engaging in potentially addictive behaviors at present do not foresee the chains that will bind them in days, weeks, months, or years to come. It is nearly always impossible to fully see what the detrimental effects of our choices will be when we first make them. This reality is written into the very structure of life itself. We need to examine our viewpoints and see where they will guide us into the future. The mists of darkness blind the eyes of men from seeing the full picture. Hence it is so important to carefully consider the principles to which we are subscribing and values we are espousing. We need to attend to our focus, our choices, and the outcomes we are pursuing.

As humans, we are always looking somewhere, ever focusing on some task to perform, forever anticipating a future that lies before us. We all have faith in the sense that the future is yet unknown, the territory is yet unexplored, the outcomes are not yet perceived. We trust in outcomes we hope to attain. However, it is evident that God does see things we cannot and guides us through the darkness to a bliss only known to those willing to trust Him. The adversary knows that following him leads to dangerous places that we rarely if ever perceive initially. We are wise to place our trust in God and believe in His directives. It is so essential that we develop this discerning capacity to take the long-term view because our happiness depends upon it. It is the deep and long-term capacity to change our limiting viewpoints in favor of divine vantage points that will help us come to Christ. This capacity will also help us to aid others in their journeys.

Intentionally choosing to dedicate our future to God *now* will make such a significant difference in our lives. One of the ways we can give a gift to God of our faith, our trust, our belief, our confidence, our agency, and our life is to deliberately look into the future that awaits us as we live righteously. By this means, we can anticipate in our imagination the great joy that will yet come to us in mortality, in the spirit world, and in the kingdom of glory that we will eventually be assigned to. We are determining that rather than follow our own will, the voice of the worldly crowd, or the fads and fashions of the moment, we will deliberately gift our future to God. This is no easy task, but our discipleship will be much easier if we do not have to continually revise our choices based on obstacles we never considered, problems we had not anticipated, or trials we never expected to confront. Whether we have concerns over Church history, changing world conditions, new scientific discoveries, or new philosophical viewpoints, I am convinced that God knew that all these things would confront us. He has prepared a way for us to navigate this challenging terrain by dedicating our devotion to Him in advance.

Take the Long View

There are three great estates in the eternal plan of salvation of our Father in Heaven. These are the first estate (premortality), the second estate (mortality and the spirit world), and the third estate (the Resurrection, Final Judgment, and assignment to a kingdom of glory) (see Abraham 3; Moses 1–3; Alma 40–42; Doctrine and Covenants 76; 88). These estates are essentially distinct places or conditions of being. They are a legacy, a gift, and an endowment from our Father in Heaven. They give us an opportunity to grow and develop in certain ways before we move on to the next stage of our development.

Our first estate involved our existence as co-eternal intelligences and as spirit daughters and sons of our heavenly parents. Each of us was created in the image and likeness of God.

Our second estate involves a time of testing in a period of probation. All mortal beings live in the second estate. In addition, the spirit world that follows mortal death is really part of the second estate. This is because in the world of spirits, we are still subject to the conditions imposed upon us by the Fall of Adam and Eve in that we are subject to mortal death—the separation of the physical body from the eternal spirit. In addition, many spirits are still subject to the separation from God that came from the Fall, which is called spiritual death. While the time of testing for faithful covenant disciples ends at mortal death (see Alma 40–42), they are still subject to physical death in the spirit world. Other spirits are still subject to both physical and spiritual death in the spirit world. In essence, these other spirits are still under a period of probation until they learn, accept, and live the doctrines, ordinances, and covenants of Christ in the world of spirits. Then they move from prison to paradise in the sense of entering the rest of God (Doctrine and Covenants 138). However, they are still in bondage in the sense of not having their physical bodies united with their eternal spirits yet. The scriptures do not seem to indicate that our premortal memory is restored to us in our second estate. This preserves the notion of it being a probationary time of testing and faith.

The third estate is where all persons get their physical bodies back—except then it will be in a condition of permanent union with their spirits. We are judged according to the desires, thoughts, words, and deeds of our lives in the second estate (meaning both mortality and the spirit world). We are then assigned to a kingdom of glory suited to that level of Christ's light that we have determined to follow. As far as I can tell, it is only at this time that we receive a full recollection of our first estate (see Alma 40–43). Our bodily glory will be contingent on our faithfulness. Similarly, our access and closeness to God will be related to our choices and deepest longings. Eternity will bring the everlasting blessings of God upon us, to the extent we have been willing to receive them.

How important it is therefore to use our time and energy now, in this very hour and day, to choose to fully follow God! This will allow us to receive the highest rewards of which we are capable. All these rich treasures are only possible through the love and power of God, His Son Jesus Christ, and the Holy Ghost.

Given that our premortal estate has already concluded (because we are here in mortality), we cannot change the choices we made during that time. We do know that we chose to follow the plan of our Father in that first estate, which is why we are here now. That should give us great encouragement to believe that we did live well in that estate. We were faithful and true to our God. We used our talents to bless the other spirits around us. We offered our gifts to God in that first place (see Alma 13). I am grateful that we have already offered the gift of our premortal life to God. Think of that! In that life before this one, we joyfully anticipated mortality and immortality. We did not choose to follow the adversary of our souls. We rejected his accusations. He countered his doubts. We dismissed his temptations. We prevailed over his deception. Our joy was found in belief. We trusted in God. We wanted to become mortal. We had confidence that with the help of God, we could choose to follow Christ even though it would be difficult. We proved ourselves by having a long-term perspective. We were more interested in growth than we were in guarantees. We were willing to take risks. Our development was more important than our safety, our progress more interesting that our ease, our opportunities more inviting than our security. We had true faith that all would be well if we did the right thing. So we have already dedicated our first estate to God. I believe that estate was a great privilege, a prized anticipation to us. It was a vital testing ground, and we passed the test. Let us take hope from the fact that we passed the first of our great tests with a decisive choice and a conclusive victory.

Of course, we still have mortality and the spirit world (estate two) and then the eternities (estate three) to consider. Let us ponder some ways in which we can use these two estates to perform and accomplish the work of God. Surely God will rejoice in the giving of these sacred gifts of time to Him and His cause.

Choose a Spiritual Focus in Mortal Life

Our focus in this life is tremendously important. What we look for so often determines what we find. What we seek powerfully impacts what we see. Where we gaze significantly shapes our perspective. I am convinced that looking to the Lord Jesus Christ as the mighty hero of our lives is a crucially important decision for each one of us. The quality of our lives is greatly impacted by this pivotal choice to look to the Lord as the example of how to live the good life. The fullness of life He offers us is beyond our present capacity to conceive.

The revelations teach us that the word of God is always good. God's truths are uplifting and edifying. They produce good results and make a positive difference. They benefit us greatly. Armed with the word of God, we can overcome our fallen nature. True doctrine is powerful in giving us the understanding and drive we need to surmount difficulty and rise toward our eternal destiny. We are not condemned to remaining stuck in the poor performance of the past. God will help us grow beyond our mistakes and errors. His laws are ones of growth, development, and progress. Let us have a mindset of spiritual growth, as this is our divine birthright. Great joy attends becoming what we are destined to become in God's beautiful plan of growth.

Each new day, new week, new month, and new year provides an opportunity to start again, to have a new beginning. We can make incremental yet significant progress in the things of the soul. Of course, there will be many hurdles to overcome. However, there can also be triumphs. We can brush away the cobwebs, clear away the clutter, and prepare for wonderful opportunities.

One of the useful principles I have learned from the restored gospel is the importance of using our capacity for imaginative vision to propel ourselves forward in spiritual things. Having a sense of looking forward with spiritual vision will allow us to see the perfection Christ plans to bring about in our lives before it becomes a reality. Consequently, we can ask ourselves:

- What spiritual messages did I hear years ago that are more relevant today than they were then?
- What warnings are gaining momentum through the passage of time?
- What doctrines understood and lived now will bless me with protection from evil and grant me righteous empowerment for the future (see 1 Nephi 14:14)?
- What prophetic pronouncements seem of lesser importance now but will be of vital relevance in years to come?
- What powerful promises were made to us in the past that we need to rely on now to endure the difficulties we are facing?
- What solid truths should we incorporate into our lives now so that they will help us to stand with faith and courage when we face terrible trouble twenty years from now?
- What practices have we followed in the past that have made our homes more holy now?
- What self-reliance principles can we apply now that will strengthen our security ten years from now?
- What commandments and covenants have we obeyed in times past that we can use to draw on the power of Christ now for ourselves and others in deep need (see Doctrine and Covenants 121)?

I believe that as we sincerely come to Christ with a desire to be made perfect through Him and to ask Him to help us to bring others to Him, something marvelous happens to us. We obtain:

- The ability to break down the walls of opposition
- Strength to dismantle the false traditions we have inherited
- A desire to overcome weakness, fears, and doubts
- The capacity to become untangled from the shackles of bondage that enslave us
- Power to become free from untruths, disabling behaviors, and self-defeating habits
- The capability to rise to a new abundant mindset

We also gain special gifts to enable us to help others draw close to Christ themselves. We are empowered with the knowledge to influence others to come unto Christ and be made new in Him.

Believe in the World of Spirits

In times when death is all around us, and we are confronted on every hand by the frailties of mortality, there is a message of hope to consider. Though we are deeply saddened when our loved ones pass away, and we ourselves will one day face physical death, we know that this is not the end of the story. Some suppose that this life is all there is, that we cease to exist when we take our final mortal breath. However, the revealed word of God says differently. We have a God who knows about life in all its marvelous richness. He has prepared a sure way for death to be overcome, for the grave to be transcended, for mortality to yield to immortality. Christ is the Resurrection and the Life (see John 11:25). Every soul that has sojourned on this earth will continue to live in spirit form upon mortal death. In addition, each person will know Resurrection through the Lord of Life. This is a message of comfort, peace, beauty, and truth (see Alma 40). We can choose now to believe in an afterlife and prepare to live well in that place of transition between mortality and immortality.

Prepare Now for an Eternity of Celestial Heaven

To offer our eternity to the Lord is to choose His everlasting path. As His course is one eternal round, our path can be likewise. We can walk the road of righteousness, not simply for a time but for always. We can choose to offer our gifts to the eternal God for His everlasting purposes. This is a supreme dedication. To say that we will worship God everlastingly is to commit the greatest possible offering we could ever make. It is to commit ourselves not only for seventy years in this mortal life but for the time we will yet live in the spirit world and the endless duration of the infinite life that only occurs in eternity. Clearly, such an offering is made in faith, as we cannot yet conceive what eternity involves with complete knowledge. We project our minds into the imagination of futurity and devote our energies, abilities, and capacities—including gifts and treasures we do not yet possess—to the glorious work of God in eternal realms.

We anticipate marvelous happenings in the eternal world to come. We expect unexpected blessings, unimagined privileges, new opportunities, and grand designs. We expect to rise to new heights, to perform additional labors, and to acquire extra proficiencies. We are therefore pledging our future unseen experiences to the great work of salvation. This is a mighty offering. Surely our Father in Heaven will honor us with great and majestic blessings as we commit to bring others to salvation as an eternal work, a lasting vocation, a ministry that never ends. "But as it is written, Eye hath not seen, nor ear heard, neither have entered into the heart of man, the things which God hath prepared for them that love him" (1 Corinthians 2:9). Let us then determine to love Him with all our souls!

The celestial heaven is a place of plentiful bounty, beautiful peace, lasting joy, jubilant love, abiding mercy, and miraculous abundance. Think of the best place you can imagine. The highest heaven is far better than this. It contains scenic beauty beyond our present visualization and ability to describe. Heaven is a place of no regrets, no illness, no disease, no remorse, no hatred, no conflict, no famine, no crime, and no war. Think of the kindest, sweetest, gentlest, noblest person you know. Heaven is the place where everyone is like this. Think of the most exquisite food, most stirring music, most wonderful literature, most poignant art, and most striking sculpting. Heaven contains all this and much more. Heaven is the place we will get to stay in forever. We won't need to leave. It will be an eternal paradise of peace, a place of everlasting belonging, and a domain of enduring happiness. It therefore makes sense that as we anticipate offering our greatest gifts to God and His children, we become ready to dwell in a place of the ultimate gifts, the greatest offerings, and the most sublime experiences (see Doctrine and Covenants 76:50–70).

14

Enter into the Fellowship of Christ

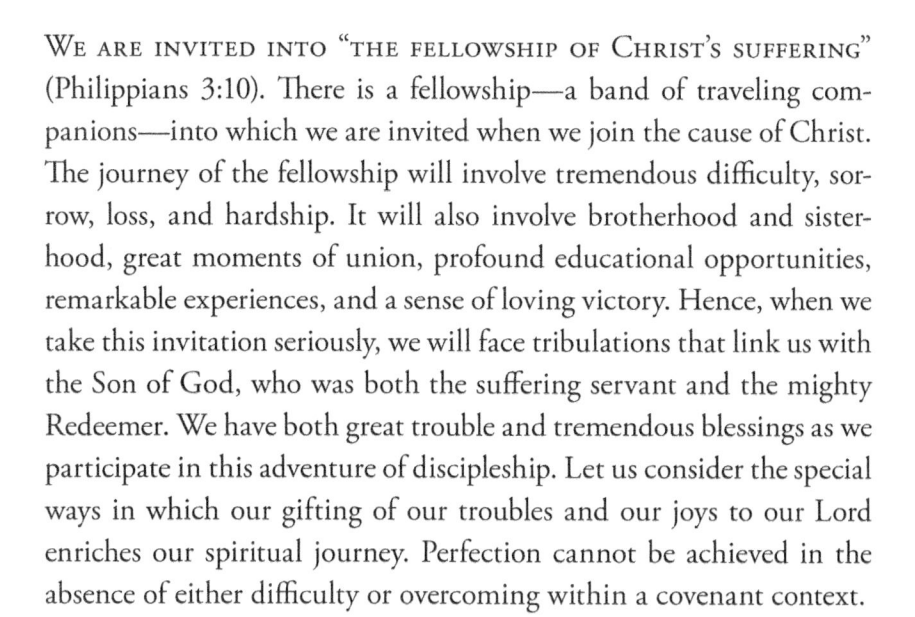

We are invited into "the fellowship of Christ's suffering" (Philippians 3:10). There is a fellowship—a band of traveling companions—into which we are invited when we join the cause of Christ. The journey of the fellowship will involve tremendous difficulty, sorrow, loss, and hardship. It will also involve brotherhood and sisterhood, great moments of union, profound educational opportunities, remarkable experiences, and a sense of loving victory. Hence, when we take this invitation seriously, we will face tribulations that link us with the Son of God, who was both the suffering servant and the mighty Redeemer. We have both great trouble and tremendous blessings as we participate in this adventure of discipleship. Let us consider the special ways in which our gifting of our troubles and our joys to our Lord enriches our spiritual journey. Perfection cannot be achieved in the absence of either difficulty or overcoming within a covenant context.

Take the Covenant Path of Christ

The covenant path is the path of Jesus Christ. His path is the way of prophets. It is the road of Saints. God will never veer from the path, nor can He break His covenant. How important it is that we strive to come onto and stay on this path of promise. If we have strayed, it is vital that we repent and return. To come to Him by means of covenant is to partake of His trouble and to know His glory. We take upon ourselves His name by covenant, which is to say we take upon ourselves both a measure of His trouble and a portion of His triumph. As He was a man of sorrows, so must we be to some extent. As He was a man of joy, we likewise must know the true joy that comes from fellowship with Him. We travel the same path, experience the same covenants and ordinances, face similar persecutions, and rejoice in the same victories. We come to know hardship and love just like our Master. The path of affliction and nobility is one we share with our Lord.

The path is strait and narrow. I think this means that it is well-defined—it has a clear purpose and focus. It requires discipline, hard work, self-sacrifice, and devotion. We all struggle with some of the requirements of discipleship at times. We have all made missteps, erred in understanding, and made mistakes of judgment. I know I have fumbled many times on my journey, sometimes inadvertently and at other times intentionally. I have been shortsighted, foolish, selfish, and sinful. I also know what it means to struggle against my own weakness, to resist evil, to try to do better. Of course, the path requires attention to righteous character. This is to be built into the fabric of our souls over time. In this sense, this path to salvation involves a covenant of character attributes in addition to certain beliefs and works.

Our character is tested in the furnace of affliction. Our resolve is tried, our determination is scrutinized, and our understanding comes under pressure. It is important that we develop long-term vision of our end goal. It is also essential that we foster faith in God, durable patience, resilient temperance, and "courage under fire." The nature of the covenant of Christ is such that it will make heavy demands and stretch the resources of even the best and noblest souls. We should not expect it to be otherwise. The covenant path inevitably involves highs and lows, disappointments and joys, obstacles and miracles. It is a path of learning, experience, and exhilarating views.

I belong to Christ as a covenant member of His Church. I belong with my Father in Heaven as I align myself with the covenant of His Son. The covenants I have made with God are powerfully impactful in my life. They give me a sense of knowing what is expected of me. The covenants are a shield and a protection to me in the sense that they safeguard me from the worst excesses of the natural man. They help me detect those who are my enemies. If someone invites or entices me to break my covenants, then I know their invitation is not inspired of God. I have faith in the promises associated with covenant keeping. Indeed, my faith is sure and steadfast because I know the true source of my covenant blessings.

Turn Suffering to Relief

I remember when I had emergency major surgery for a ruptured small intestine in December 2010. I woke up in the intensive care unit and was feeling the effects of pain, immobility, disorientation, strong painkiller drugs, sadness, and so on. One of the things that really helped during that time was the kind personal attention of the nurses who treated me. They were excellent at providing nurturing care, encouragement, attention to detail, and conscientious regard. I was very touched by their efforts. Weeks later when I was leaving the hospital, I sought them out and thanked them for their kindness. They responded that they were simply doing their job. They obviously did not feel they had done anything out of the ordinary in their service. I appreciate that vantage point, but the situation looked very different to me. I was impacted by their caring attention in a profound, personal way. I was in desperate need. I was ailing. I was sick, sore, and in need of help. I got the help I needed, and I really appreciated it.

To them it was routine. To me it was essential, healing, and so important. I felt very grateful for it because I was not able to do for myself what they were able to do for me. Although I was suffering, they made efforts to relief my suffering, to calm my fears, to restore me to health. This was an experience of a lifetime. I saw nursing in a whole different way. I saw it from the vantage point of being someone in exhaustion, distress, hunger, thirst, and loneliness. Their efforts to meet my needs were full and rich. I felt cared for, looked after, minded, and highly regarded. I felt served. I just do not have the words to explain the crucial role that this form of ministering played to my urgent and immediate needs. It was lifesaving to me, not just physically but also emotionally. I likewise felt great uplift from the members of the Church who came to visit me and console me in affliction. My family, of course, played the greatest role in being constant and considerate in looking after me at that time. I learned in a way I never knew before what real help looks like and how it feels. I wish everyone could have that experience of being assisted in a stark time of trouble. I believe it would give many people a very different perspective about what it means to have someone stretch themselves to meet the pressing personal requirements of another person in a time of dire need.

Suffering is not without significance or meaning. It has a vital role to play in perfecting us. What function do pain and suffering have in the perfecting process? Pain is not pleasant. It is uncomfortable. However, it can educate us. It can instruct us in ways that pleasure cannot. It can show us that we need to pay attention to something we have been avoiding or overlooking, to do something different in our lives, to change our focus. It can help us to look outward to the difficulties of others so that we might seek to lighten their load. Obviously, there would be little need for us to stretch ourselves to assist others if serious troubles never arose. For example, consider the following:

- Storms, floods, hurricanes, mudslides, earthquakes, tsunamis, fires, and so on are opportunities for each of us to act in needful ways in helping those impacted by such natural disasters.
- Hospitals and care homes are not just occupied by the sick and infirm. They are visited millions of times each day by concerned family members and friends. When our thoughts and feelings turn to those who are sick and afflicted, we spend less time thinking of our own wishes and troubles and more time trying to look after others. This outreach is a good thing. I believe it is a necessary thing.

As I read the example of Lehi being led through the darkness to the light, I can see that difficulty can lead us to God in a way that nothing else can. I see the man in white who comes to Lehi as a true messenger—the Savior or an angel—leading Lehi from the dark and dreary wilderness (this telestial, fallen world) through the dark and dreary waste (the terrain of the adversary's desolating influence). The heavenly messenger is guiding him through the inevitable parts of this fallen world—darkness (confusion) and dreariness (sadness, loneliness)—to bring him in due course to a better place. He is leading him to the Tree of Life. This takes time and patience, even when heavenly messengers are leading us. The heavenly messenger does not remove the need for Lehi to keep focused on moving forward in faith. The messenger does not banish the darkness or dreariness—he just ensures Lehi can get through it. The messenger does not dissolve the need for Lehi to seek comfort and help from the Father through prayer. The Savior or an angel does not tell us not to pray.

Heavenly beings guide us, but that does not mean we will not feel some fear or trepidation during the journey. Let's face it—being on the strait and narrow path does not automatically remove feelings of sorrow or worry. God consoles us by giving us guidance, but we still need to find our way through the mist of darkness. I think Lehi had to pass through these challenging places before he could really come to the Tree of Life. He passed through this darkness to learn by his own experience what spiritual bitterness feels like. He could appreciate the value of the tree most fully only by contrasting it with the time he spent in a measure of darkness. He sought mercy from God, and God gave him mercy. Some of the feelings Lehi had related to being a traveler in a lone and weary world. Adam also received visits from angels, but he still had to pray to God. We need all the divine guidance we can get in this world!

We can be a guide to others in their dark times. We can point the way to the Tree of Life. We can encourage others to pray to God for mercy. We can instill in others a trust of prophets, seers, and revelators. We can invite others to follow God, especially when they find themselves in dark times. God is pleased when the gifts we receive from Him are used by us to become a gift to others. When we receive mercy from God, we can speak of Him in grateful terms. When we are divinely led, we can bear testimony of that truth. When we find light and hope, we can speak to others about how such discovery is possible in their lives too.

Transform Dismissiveness into Attentiveness

I have thought much about my greatest fear. If I were to meet the Savior and He betrayed me—insulted, ignored, belittled, mocked, laughed at me—it would be the worst disappointment I could face. It would be the ultimate dejection to be dismissed by God Himself. To be overlooked or viewed condescendingly by the One I rejoice in, admire, look to, and place my trust in would be an ordeal of terrible proportions. It would be galling, hurtful, and painful beyond all. If that ever were to happen as a form of testing, I hope I would forgive freely and completely. Then I would know that nothing can defeat or overcome me. It would be my greatest victory. I think this worry gets to the heart of all suffering. We feel it is unfair, undeserved, and undesirable. We may feel humiliated, walked over, despised, or misunderstood. This is especially true in relationships that are fractured.

Of course, I know that Christ does not ignore us. He teaches us that He will listen to us. If all others abandon us, He will not. He will hear our voice and know our names. He will empower us through paying attention to us. While some may ignore us, He will not. He brings us to Him. He walks with us, talks with us, teaches us, and cares for us. How empowering His listening is! His attentiveness causes us to rejoice. In like manner, we can replace any tendency we have to ignore others into a willingness to attend to them. Our personal attention to them will point them to Christ as the great source of their interest.

Change Accusations into Affirmations

I have noticed that our world is increasingly immersed in a spirit of accusation. Especially the Church and kingdom of our God is harassed with all sorts of wild accusations. Where does this spirit come from? The revelations tell us:

> And there was war in heaven: Michael and his angels fought against the dragon; and the dragon fought and his angels,
>
> And prevailed not; neither was their place found any more in heaven.
>
> And the great dragon was cast out, that old serpent, called the Devil, and Satan, which deceiveth the whole world: he was cast out into the earth, and his angels were cast out with him.
>
> And I heard a loud voice saying in heaven, Now is come salvation, and strength, and the kingdom of our God, and the power of his Christ: for *the accuser of our brethren* is cast down, which *accused them before our God day and night.*
>
> And they overcame him by the blood of the Lamb, and by the word of their testimony; and they loved not their lives unto the death. (Revelation 12:7–11; emphasis added)

In other words, in the spiritual war fought before this world was, there were the hosts of heaven—those who sided with the Father and the Son—and there were also those who followed the dragon—he who sought to burn all that is holy. The devil is the "accuser" of the brethren. That means that Lucifer accused the Father and Jehovah of all sorts of pernicious motives. He was trying to attribute to them his own despicable contempt. He accused the noble and great ones of not caring about their brothers and sisters. He accused them of taking unwarranted risks by granting people agency. He spoke against Michael, Enoch, Noah, Abraham, Moses, and Joseph Smith. He was antagonistic toward Peter, James, and John. He accused the Brethren of not caring, not loving, not showing compassion. Does any of this sound familiar?

I note that there was a way to resist the deception of the devil in that premortal world. Those who overcame the devil did so by the blood of the Lamb and by the word of their testimony. They relied on the saving sacrifice of Jehovah. They believed in His atoning redemption. They spoke of His love, His goodness, and His reliability. They bore testimony that He was the Lamb without blemish, that He would be the blood-stained soul who would take upon Himself the sins, pain, sorrows, and death of all the world. They believed in Him and let their faith in Him be known. They trusted Him. Their testimony was strong. It was not faint or fickle. They cared more about doing the right thing than doing the easy thing, the pleasurable thing, or the safe thing. They became part of the fellowship (brotherhood, bond, fraternity) of Christ. In mortality, they laid down their lives in His cause, defending His honor, speaking up for His courage, testifying of His might. This is how we turn from the accusations of the devil to the affirmations of Christ. Our Lord says we can do this. We can make it. Through believing on His pure and holy blood, we can overcome every evil, resist every deception, and hold fast to every good thing. Let us affirm to ourselves and others that Christ is the Lamb without fault or failing. He is victorious over sin and death. Let us repeat that truth so that all who hear it and believe it may be saved.

Replace Disease with Healing

We are all suffering from some type of disease—whether physical, spiritual, or emotional. We are like patients in the hospital of the great Physician. We need to take our medicine and full treatment. We are to work toward healing, even if it takes many years, like in the following cases:

- A woman suffered for twelve years with an issue of blood *before* she was healed.
- The man at the pool at Bethesda waited and watched while others were healed *before* him.
- Zeezrom had to experience the burning fever *before* He could know relief.
- Lazarus was dead for four days *before* being brought back to life.
- The ten lepers languished *before* being cleansed.
- Joseph Smith spent six months in Liberty Jail *before* finding freedom and consolation.
- Alma was tormented by his misdeeds for three days and nights *before* solace came.

All of these had to show patience and faith first. Eventually, the miracle came. There was spiritual and physical healing for those who sought it. Our once bruised, broken, and battered Savior heals all our wounds. My admiration for His divine power is pronounced. We can know Him as the great healer of our souls! We can also inspire others to look to Christ for hope and healing. Our suffering can lead us to salvation if we allow it to.

Take the Names of Christ upon Us

I am grateful to Elder Jonathan S. Schmitt of the Seventy for giving me an increased understanding of the importance of taking upon ourselves *all* the names of Jesus Christ.[8] As he taught of this important idea, it became apparent to me that we need to take upon ourselves all the many names of Christ in the sense of receiving all the attributes His names signify. We ought not to limit ourselves to acquiring only a few of His personal traits. We can instead become well-rounded in all the aspects of His being. It is worthwhile to reflect on this scriptural idea in detail.

I have also come to sense that this is part of what it means to engage in the fellowship of Christ. As we spend time with the Savior and those like Him, we rub shoulders with those who are striving to develop and emulate all His characteristics. Initially, we do not comprehend that we are called to overcome all our deficiencies. However, as we take the high road of spiritual adventure, we become more aware of our faults and shortcomings. We also become more enabled to develop—one by one and line upon line—each attribute of divinity as expressed in the many names of our Lord.

Let us consider how each of His names points to a particular aspect of His nature. We can then see more easily how our emulation of Christ is to be more than general goodness. Rather, it is to be specific and focused. Eventually, it is to become total and complete. We will also be able to detect why the scriptures use similar names and characteristics when referring both to the Lord and to His faithful covenant

---

8. See Jonathan S. Schmitt, "That They Might Know Thee," *Liahona*, Nov. 2022, 104–106.

people. This also means that we will be able to use any new qualities we develop by focusing on all the names of Christ in a way that honors our Savior and leads others to Him. Hence, this is part of the gift that we can offer in His service.

His Names and Titles	Associated Attributes	Our Names and Titles	Associated Attributes
Jehovah, Great I AM	Godhood, permanence	Co-eternal with God	Eternality of identity
Creator	Creative, life-loving	Co-creators with God	Designers, crafters, inventors, artists
Christ, Messiah, Anointed One	Chosen for special purposes	Covenant people, anointed ones	Loyal to a sacred cause
Wonderful	Incorporates that which is optimally inspiring	People of God, a peculiar people, Saints	Designated to be set apart from the world
Counselor	The giver of wise advice	Counselors, advisors	Called to share truth with all in love
Only Begotten Son of God	Embodies the nature of the Father	Sons and daughters of God	Divine nature
Son of Man of Holiness	Direct offspring of the Supreme Being	Children of promise	Born to represent God's love to the world
Emmanuel	Represents the Godhead to the rest of humanity	Names given by revelation such as Michael, Joseph	Commissioned to bring holy gifts to the world

Mighty God	Powerful	Mighty men and women	Able to do otherwise impossible things
Holy One of Israel	Uniquely designated to represent the covenant family	A holy nation, sanctified men and women	Commanded to be a light to the world
Lamb of God	Unblemished and willing	Servants	Called to serve all of humanity
Savior	Saves from sin and death	Saviors on Mount Zion	Called to offer salvation to all
Redeemer	Brings to full fruition	Messengers of the covenant	Offer exaltation to God's children
Deliverer	Rescues all others	Captains in the army of the Lord	Interested in each soul and all souls
Mediator	Reconciles all to God	Covenant disciples	Want to bring every soul to God
Advocate	Intervenes to assist others	Helpers	Willing to serve the one
Prince of Peace	Brings everlasting inner and outer peace	Peacemakers	Want to bring peace to the entire world
Lord of lords	Master of dignity	Lords	Organizers, administrators, leaders, planners

King of kings	Leader of greatest nobility	A royal people, kings and queens unto the Most High God	A people that knows about duty, honor, and responsibility
Everlasting Father	Makes spiritual rebirth possible for the children of God	Patriarchs and matriarchs	Brings life to people, ideas, and places
Good Shepherd	Always cares for the sheep	Shepherds to the flock	Watching, overseeing, ministering
Lord	Holds authority over all men	Presiding officers, key-holders, leaders	Envisioning, leading, delegating, empowering
Lord of Hosts	Responsible to guide all men to salvation	Captains of tens and fifties	Prepared to do what is needed
Judge	Perfectly holds all people accountable for their lives	Common judges in Israel	Wisdom, discernment, holding accountable

To come into covenant friendship with Christ is to both suffer for His cause and also to rejoice like He does. Let us offer both our afflictions and our joys up to Him in sacred token of His great offering. Our suffering will sanctify ourselves and others. Our happiness will bless both ourselves and others.

15

Minister to the Holy One

Now let's turn our focus toward another significant offering to God: sincere service to a single soul. This offering is in stark contrast to worldly viewpoints that focus on different ambitions. As a boy, I often viewed service in terms of magnitude, scale, and scope. The more visible the service and the greater the number of people impacted, the more important the service appeared to me to be. I was also inordinately impressed by status:

- I was impressed by epic movies where heroes performed daring acts of bravery.
- I was in awe at Olympic athletes showing amazingly honed skills on the world stage.
- I admired the rich and famous and their splendid, grand, and lavish lives.
- I valued ceremonial acts where individuals were set apart for positions of prominence, such as the coronations of kings and queens.
- I thought men who were physically strong were the paragon of virtue. Women who were beautiful could do no wrong.

This view has some merit. Many of these persons have worked hard, mastered their craft, and brought great joy to millions of people through their accomplishments. And even in spiritual terms, there is much to be said for narratives that convey a sense of cosmic proportions. After all, the Creation, Fall, and Atonement impact billions of people. Such events play a very significant role in God's plan. In addition, they were performed by a small number of people—certainly the Fall of Adam and Eve and the Atonement of Christ were. Some events clearly have a marked influence upon the world. They are special happenings and require extraordinary efforts to bring them to pass. Some individuals perform mighty works that differ from the usual efforts of most of us who are seemingly ordinary humans.

When I was seventeen, I was preparing to be a missionary. I thought how great it would be to be an assistant to the mission president as a missionary because then I would be noticed and admired by others. This was a complete misunderstanding of the role of leadership. Interestingly, apart from the twelve days I spent as district leader in the missionary training center and the two months I spent as a trainer of a fellow missionary, I was not called to be a leader in the mission field. This taught me a measure of humility. Some other missionaries aspired to leadership as I did. Some of them got opportunities and some of them did not. However, I noticed that those who aspired to leadership struggled to overcome their desires for "ascendancy."

This is not a criticism of them since I also had similar misplaced desires. Instead, it is as reflection on the inherent dangers of wanting position as a means of elevating ourselves above others. That is a recipe for tragedy. It's far better to humble ourselves and come to know that leadership is an opportunity to serve and is genuinely a refining process. Of course, although as young missionaries we sometimes had weaknesses (including ones very apparent to others), we also performed much service and learned many important lessons. We all have a mixture of strength and weakness inside of us. It takes time and experience to polish our souls. Many years later as a branch president, I tried to focus on service to the individual as the hallmark of my ministry. It is not about prominence. It is about love of others. That can be a difficult lesson to learn, but it is so important.

As I matured, I came to see very differently. It is not that the desire for a large-scale impact is fundamentally flawed. However, the notoriety we give to many perceived successes may come to take on a different meaning when we see that some individuals may be grossly dishonest or selfishly motivated. Of course, all humans are subject to the temptation to seek our own perceived interest over the good of others. The appearance of great achievement may not always match the reality behind it. Nor do individuals who achieve "great" things in the world always have easy or happy lives. They often struggle with many shortcomings that come to define them more than accomplishments of great renown.

This is not to say that God does not work through those who are flawed. It does, however, point to the dangers of seeking for great accomplishment or great visibility without being simultaneously grounded in personal morality so that our alignment with God is ever-present in our lives. Such anchoring becomes more important when we are given great responsibility, enhanced status, or public prominence. We are often tested to the deepest degree by the outcomes we thought we desired. As the wise adage goes, "Be careful what you wish for because you might just get it."

I have discerned that many very important and significant events occur on a much smaller scale. While not as dramatic or noticeable as large events, they nonetheless find significance in the gospel plan of our Father and His Son. This is because they have an impact on the person or persons involved. This influence may be small, but it is impactful. It can have a domino result, a contagion effect, an important outcome. The consistency of small deeds performed well over a long period of time amounts to great things in the timetable of God.

There is a protective element with small-scale, one-to-one service. It is far less visible. Therefore, there is far less temptation to have corrupt motives in performing such works. Of course, such service is not immune from corruption. However, it is a great way of keeping our motives in check if we ask ourselves, "How can I keep this service confidential so that I am not contaminated by a desire for praise or glory?"

Let us consider that Mary, the mother of Jesus, cared for Him when He was a newborn babe. She nourished Him as a little child. This was long before people knew who He was. No doubt she washed Him, fed Him, clothed Him, instructed Him, and nurtured Him! This was small, quiet service. Did the Son of God appreciate that service? Unquestionably yes—certainly when He got older. This was "one to one" help and love. And what of the woman who anointed the Savior's feet with oil? This service was not done for praise or notoriety. In fact, Simon did not appreciate her service and called attention to the "type" of woman she was. This was genuine service given in love. It was intentional and purposeful. The Savior appreciated it greatly.

I hope that each one of us has opportunities to serve other individuals in simple ways that mean much to them. We can remind people that they are noticed by us, that we remember them, and that we are aware of them. This is small but significant service in God's eyes.

The sacred serving of one soul is a marvelous opportunity for each of us to calibrate our spiritual desires. Some questions that come to us as we seek to serve in secret sacredness are these:

- Would I do this act if only one person benefited from it?
- What are the real and deep needs of this person I am seeking to bless?
- What are the hidden wounds I might be able to relieve to some degree?
- How can I use my specific gifts and talents to show genuine concern for this one person I desire to help?
- How can I ensure that I am more concerned with meeting their needs than I am with meeting my own in this service?

We may be tempted to believe that the serving of one person is a small or insignificant matter. However, to serve one is to serve everyone. The Lord has been trying to teach me about the importance of the "one" for many years:

- I have felt unique and special during ordinances I have personally received. He has shown me great love and regard even when I thought little of myself.
- I baptized only one person as a missionary. Two years to save one soul may seem like a waste of time, but in the economy of heaven, to save one soul is an eternal blessing for that soul and so is well worth the time spent.
- I only had one child. Having had much opportunity to work with my son personally in many types of experiences has been a further education on the deep importance that individual persons hold to God.

I love the truth that Alma the Elder was reclaimed by one man, Abinadi, so that he could then go forward to bless and save others one by one. God told him, "Thou art my servant; and I covenant with thee that thou shalt have eternal life; and thou shalt *serve me* and go forth in my name, and shalt *gather together* my sheep" (Mosiah 26:20; emphasis added).

God knew who Alma the Elder was! He knew his propensity to serve God. He knew his desire to bring the sheep to the spiritual rescue. God covenanted with Alma that he would obtain eternal life. This was a personal promise to the one. God saw one soul and knew that his heart, desires, and inclinations were righteous and faithful. For God to recognize and specify to Alma that he was a faithful servant must have brought a measure of great comfort to Alma. Even if others in high places such as King Noah did not hear his words, God knew and saw him for who he truly was. God knows the thoughts and intents of our hearts. He knows when we have these good desires to do His will and serve Him. He values our commitment, resolve, and integrity in seeking to be firm in our faith and loyal to the cause we have chosen. He rewards our genuine seeking with precious outpourings.

I love the account of Alma at the waters of Mormon. Each child of God taught by Alma was baptized in the name of the Lord. Each made an individual covenant, and each came to regard that special place in sacred terms. What happened there made the place holy:

> And it came to pass that he said unto them: Behold, here are the waters of Mormon (for thus were they called) and now, as ye are a desirous to come into the fold of God, and to be called his people, and are *willing to bear one another's burdens*, that they may be light;
>
> Yea, and are a *willing to mourn with those that mourn*; yea, and *comfort those that stand in need of comfort*, and to stand as *witnesses of God* at all times and in all things, and in all places that ye may be in, even until death, that ye may be redeemed of God, and be numbered with those of the first resurrection, that ye may have eternal life—
>
> Now I say unto you, if this be the desire of your hearts, what have you against being baptized in the name of the Lord, as a witness before him that ye have entered into a covenant with him, that ye will *serve him* and keep his commandments, that he may pour out his Spirit more abundantly upon you? (Mosiah 18:8–10; emphasis added)

This baptismal covenant is a relational one of bearing the burdens of others. A covenant to mourn with the sad and encourage the despondent. To build memories in sacred places as we share spiritual experiences together. To go forward with a determination to be of service to those around us. It is evident that our baptismal covenants involve both God and our brothers and sisters. We covenant to serve, to lighten loads, and to be connected to others in compassionate strengthening. We promise to bless, lift, and uplift. That holy covenant, made in a memorable setting, is a powerful reminder of our willingness and ability to be a source of consolation to others, one person at a time, one conversation at a time, one text message at a time, one phone call at a time, and one day at a time. We are covenant servants!

As Christ served the one, so can we:

- He served Jairus and his daughter.
- He opened the eyes of *one* poor blind man.
- He healed ten lepers, *one by one*.
- He walked a long distance to raise *one* man from death—Lazarus.
- He traveled far to comfort *two* grieving sisters—Mary and Martha.

- He spoke privately to a confused Nicodemus.
- He spent time to discuss life-changing truths with *one* woman at a well of water.

Minister to the Wounded Christ

When Christ was in the Garden of Gethsemane, He began to experience a burden of grief and pain that surpassed anything He had previously known. His suffering was beyond compare. He said to His closest associates in His extremity, "Could you not watch with me one hour?" (Matthew 26:40) Was that too much to ask, too difficult to expect, too onerous a burden to carry? Could mortal men meaningfully assist their overburdened Lord? Whatever the possibilities, we know that the tiredness of the Apostles pushed them into slumber. Not so for Christ. He was acutely aware of His suffering. We know that an angel of strength appeared to Christ (see Luke 22:43).

Let us ponder that. What does it mean that an angel came to give Him strength? Well, part of the office of the ministry of angels is "to fulfil and to do the work of the covenants of the Father" (Moroni 7:31). In this connection, I believe this is a great example of the baptismal covenant we have just been discussing. This angel came to help Christ bear the most terrible burden He would ever experience. He came to bring comfort and support. He came to bring desperate help in a time of need. We do not know who this angel was. However, if he came to bring strength, then he must have had a great degree of strength. This was a mighty servant and angel of God. Most likely this was someone of great spiritual standing. Perhaps it was Adam (Michael) or Noah (Gabriel) or Enoch (who may be the angel Raphael). Whoever it was, I believe they succeeded in their mission. No doubt Christ felt that this visitation was a moment of mercy. He surely felt sustained in His mighty priesthood errand by this powerful messenger. I have asked myself the following questions:

- What words were spoken by this strong messenger?
- Was a priesthood blessing of comfort offered?
- Was a prayer of strength said on Christ's behalf?

- Was an embrace given, a kiss bestowed?
- Was a hymn sung?

I think if we had the opportunity to do likewise, it would be a precious opportunity. If we were the angel who had visited Christ in His exhausting despair, what would we have said or done to ease His pain, lift His spirits, console His soul, and encourage Him onward? You might ponder that and think about what good gifts you could have offered in His cause. Let these motivations and talents be a source of inspiration to you as you seek to minister.

My life is a testament to the saving power of the Lord Jesus Christ. Anxiety has often washed over me like a flood—that nervous tension that restricts breathing and constrains peace. Perturbed, disturbed, worried—I have been there regularly and consistently. I have known the shadows, the self-doubt, the fear of conflict, the angst associated with vulnerability, the trepidation of being exposed for what I was—weak, insecure, frightened!

I know that I feel peace only because He was chastised, that my consolation comes because of His affliction, that forgiveness comes because He refused to be swallowed up with contempt for me. My iniquities led to His bruising; my wrongdoing injured His sweet soul. My lust is overcome through His virtue. My foolishness has given way to His wisdom. In the valley of the shadow of death, I have become acquainted with His companionship and walked by His side. He has visited me in my affliction, bound up my wounds, wiped away my tears, calmed my fears, and taken my anger from me.

I have wandered as a misled sheep. I have sometimes strayed from my noble nature. Desires for happiness placed in the wrong things have been replaced with strong impulses to follow where He leads. With His stripes I am healed. He was bruised, broken, battered, and betrayed to make me new, whole, befriended, and happy. I am not ashamed to announce His character, proclaim His destiny, mention His work, and participate in His salvation. I welcome His glory. I sustain His doctrine. I advocate His purposes. I rejoice in His saving sacrifice.

Through Him, the darkest night of my soul has been transformed into the light-filled morning of forgiveness. My life—which was muddied with sin, lost in transgression, and dampened with despair—has become new in love and light. The dark has given way to light, the hatred to love, the sorrow to joy, the confusion to clarity, the fear to courage, the ignorance to knowledge. New life is mine through Him.

The Atonement of the Lord is deeply personal to me. I have discerned that the Savior of the world knows all my sins, mistakes, and weaknesses. He has taken upon Himself my smallness of soul, my petty disgruntlements, and my selfish covetousness. He knows it all—there is no part hidden from His view and experience. Yet He stands eager to help, ready to transform, willing to change my soul. He has blotted my sins out through His generous goodness. He has redeemed my broken spirit, healed my sorrowing heart, and cured my sin sickness. He has raised me up, lifted my sights, enlarged my vision, and given me a new character. I now know something of courage, virtue, hope, love, kindness, mercy, generosity, patience, and goodness.

Does God know your inner thoughts, fears, and brokenness—yes!

Does He know your rejoicings, resolutions, and victories—surely!

We are sent to succeed in this life. We fail sometimes, but we are not sent only to falter or ultimately to fail. Given what I now know of Christ, I think and feel differently about Him. I have sometimes imagined the Savior attending sacrament meeting. I have pondered how I might cater to His needs:

- How would I pass the sacrament to Him?
- How would I teach if He were there?
- What would my prayers involve if He were in the meeting?
- What if I were called to be His ministering brother? How would I discern His real needs?
- Would my resolve to keep serving be strengthened by knowing He was relying on me to do my duty and work in His cause?

Let us consider the parable of the good Samaritan. Imagine that Christ is the traveler who fell among thieves and that you are the good

Samaritan. Let us reflect within. What would you do if you came across Him? Likely, you would not know it was your Lord. You might see Him as the "other." Your opportunity to serve Him would be tested. We are all tempted to walk by the other side. What would this experience be like? To bind His wounds, to carry Him to safety, to pay for His lodgings? To save His life? I believe you would feel honored to give your humble offerings to help Him if you recognized Him. But what if we did not recognize Him? Would we still help?

In this vein, consider how you might have ministered to Him in these circumstances:

- When He was sad, lonely, and tired
- When He was tried before the leaders of the day
- When He was beaten, spat upon, cursed, and derided
- When He was scourged and crucified

Contemplate Standing in His Stead

Let us consider another thought experiment. It is an idea that has helped me appreciate the Lord more fully. Imagine you had offered to be the Savior in the beginning. Perhaps you could never see yourself having been either able or willing to make such an offer. However, after coming to understand more fully the suffering of the Lord, and the great love He showed for you, and having placed yourself in the attitude of ministering to Him during His ordeal in the Garden of Gethsemane and during His torture and crucifixion, a shift within you happened. Your love for the Lord has grown exponentially and you have desired deeply to care for Him, love Him, serve Him, and bring Him relief from pain. You want to take His place, if only you could. Not for ambition or pride or vanity's sake, but for the sake of the great love you have for Him and others.

Obviously, this is just hypothetical. We will never have to experience an infinite and eternal Atonement. However, I believe that as we come to see how the Lord sees us, we start to see Him the same way. We have a loving tender regard for Him. We wish we could minister to Him in affliction, to wipe the blood from His brow, to give Him water to sup, to give Him a place to lay His head, to clothe His naked body, to tend to His horrific wounds, to mourn with Him, to comfort Him, to speak consoling words of support, to nourish His battered soul. As we place ourselves in His stead in our imagination, in a sense we come to see as He sees, know as He knows, and love as He loves. We would perhaps want to take the cup from Him and drink it ourselves. Now, of course, this can never happen. This was His load to carry, His burden to bear, His work to perform. As we see ourselves as one who would minister to Christ in His terrible predicament, we also come to sense the pronounced value of ministering to others.

I think this line of thinking helps to explain why Joseph Smith asked John Taylor to sing "A Poor Wayfaring Man of Grief" twice while in Carthage Jail. Joseph was being consoled by the thought that he loved his suffering Lord and would minister to Him gladly if he could. Consider the sober words:

> 1. A poor wayfaring Man of grief
> Hath often crossed me on my way,
> Who sued so humbly for relief
> That *I could never answer nay.*
> I had not pow'r to ask his name,
> Whereto he went, or whence he came;
> Yet there was something in his eye
> That won my love; I knew not why.
>
> 2. Once, when my scanty meal was spread,
> He entered; not a word he spake,
> Just perishing for want of bread.
> *I gave him all*; he blessed it, brake,
> And ate, but gave me part again.
> Mine was an angel's portion then,
> For while I fed with eager haste,
> The crust was manna to my taste.
>
> 3. I spied him where a fountain burst
> Clear from the rock; his strength was gone.
> The heedless water mocked his thirst;
> He heard it, saw it hurrying on.

I ran and raised the suff'rer up;
Thrice from the stream he drained my cup,
Dipped and returned it running o'er;
I drank and never thirsted more.

4. 'Twas night; the floods were out; it blew
A winter hurricane aloof.
I heard his voice abroad and flew
To bid him welcome to my roof.
I warmed and clothed and cheered my guest
And laid him on my couch to rest,
Then made the earth my bed and seemed
In Eden's garden while I dreamed.

5. Stript, wounded, beaten nigh to death,
I found him by the highway side.
I roused his pulse, brought back his breath,
Revived his spirit, and supplied
Wine, oil, refreshment—he was healed.
I had myself a wound concealed,
But from that hour forgot the smart,
And peace bound up my broken heart.

6. In pris'n I saw him next, condemned
To meet a traitor's doom at morn.
The tide of lying tongues I stemmed,
And honored him 'mid shame and scorn.
My friendship's utmost zeal to try,
He asked if I for him would die.
The flesh was weak; my blood ran chill,
But my free spirit cried, "I will!"

7. Then in a moment to my view
The stranger started from disguise.
The tokens in his hands I knew;
The Savior stood before mine eyes.

He spake, and my poor name he named,
"Of me thou hast not been ashamed.
These deeds shall thy memorial be;
Fear not, thou didst them unto me."[9]

I feel privileged to know with surety that Jesus is the Christ. Where do we find Christ? We find Him visiting the lonely, hungry, worried, and distressed. He brings them companionship, food, consolation, and hope. As we do likewise, we come to know Him deeply, intimately, and reassuringly. As we minister to the bruised, forgotten, overlooked, heartbroken, and forsaken among us, we will find that Christ is laboring along with us. Such a gift of empathic service will be very appreciated by Him.

---

9. "A Poor Wayfaring Man of Grief," *Hymns*, no. 29; emphasis added.

16

FILL THE ETERNAL MEASURE OF OUR CREATION

THE DIVINE PATTERN OF GIVING AND BECOMING ISN'T JUST SOMEthing that happens in this life—it extends throughout eternity. Many years ago, my wife and I took an evening course in astronomy at a local school. As we learned more about this amazing universe that houses us, we were struck by the grand design involved. The size of what surrounds us is truly impressive. Seeing patterns in the stars is not a childish activity, for the pattern of this realm of glory is only visible to us if we have eyes to see it. I am struck by the great scope and scale of this space in which we are located. Given the sheer power of huge suns of burning gas, the intricate design of spiral galaxies, the amazing speed of light, and the beautiful colors of planets such as ours, I am awestruck and inspired by the grandeur of the heavens. I, like millions before me, have looked at the glowing stars at night and been touched by a sense of infinite magnitude. What a special sight to behold!

This is not mere chance. Obviously, I understand that those who think the universe came into existence randomly can still have a rich and deep appreciation of how special it is. However, for me, I see the evidence all around me of the great and sublime intelligence of God. I see His wisdom, creativity, love of architectural expression, and great goodness manifest in His beautiful and wondrous design. This vantage point offers a sense of awe, wonder, and inspiration that the notion of a random universe cannot match.

Our God is a planning God. He has a purpose for all things that are created. His vision is not limited in the way ours often is. We may not always comprehend the full purposes for something existing, but He clearly does. It is evident that the purpose for which suns were created is to give light and heat. Stars are to shine, light is to illuminate, planets are to revolve, and moons are to impact the tides. This allows life to exist and flourish. There would be little point to having a sun in the sky that offered no radiance, or having stars that never shine or moons that never move. The sense of law that governs these material things makes life possible and somewhat predictable. Similarly, each child of God has a reason for existing. We may not yet be aware of our purposes, or we may not yet have aligned ourselves with these purposes entirely. It is important to consider what it might look like for us to sense a greater understanding of the aims of our creation.

I have been sharing my firm belief in this book that now is a great time to reflect on our possibilities. According to the divine design of God, each of us has a reason for being, a purpose for living, and a destiny to discover. It is intended that we will fill the measure of our creation, meaning that we rise to the opportunities God desires for us to achieve. We might fruitfully consider how we can cultivate the following in our mortal lives:

- A closer connection with God through intentional crafting of time spent drawing closer to Him
- Improved relationships with family and friends through loving service
- Pursuing a hobby, talent, gift, ability, or creative outlet that we are interested in developing

Of course, the full extent and meaning of our creative endowments will not become apparent in mortality. Only in the eternities can we know the full development of our potential. I want to look at how the eternities will offer opportunities for us to give our all to God in ways that are not possible in mortality. In this vein, I have often thought about the people who might be wonderful at doing certain things in this life but because of circumstances never had the opportunity:

- Those who might have been concert pianists or gifted artists who never had the chance to explore their innate gifts in this life due to early death or living in a time when such privileges were not available
- Those who might have been great teachers or superb athletes or amazing lawyers, but the opportunities were never afforded to them due to poverty, war, or other prohibitions
- Those who might have been wonderful spouses or engaged parents but because of limitations, such as intellectual impairments or physical disabilities, could not have these experiences in mortality

I have often wondered what we might be capable of if the shackles of mortal limitations were removed from us. What would happen if we were not bound down by mortal ailments, no longer opposed by antagonistic forces, no more subject to damning self-doubts, no more constrained by conflict? What might happen in our relationships if we could transcend the petty bickering, contention, jealousies, and animosities that seem to flourish everywhere among humans? What if we could trust everyone we met and they trusted us? What if bullying ceased? What if we rejoiced in the successes of others because we no longer felt threatened by them or lessened by their accomplishments? What if other people could see the good in us and we could see it in them? What if we had greater power to call forth the rich potential latent in others?

What if we no longer lost heart due to facing unrelenting obstacles a thousand times? What if our anxieties, fears, sorrows, and heartbreak were gone? What if learning disabilities were removed? What if dyslexia vanished and ADHD was no more? What if our depression was suddenly vanquished? What about the removal of locked-in syndrome, dementia, and paralysis? What if all the barriers of our weakness, error, inability, and failure were broken down? What if all the elements of our spiritual, intellectual, social, and physical nature were healed and improved? What if we received new powers of sight, sound, touch, taste, and feeling? What if we could sing in tune, visualize words in our minds, and speak the desires of our hearts with clarity and passion? What if we could now learn to play the piano, learn a new language, paint more than stick figures, and learn how to solve a Rubik's cube? What poems would we write, what words could we speak, what songs would we sing, what praise would we offer, what joys would we feel, and what relationships would we nourish if the chains of our limitation were removed from us?

I foresee a day when these seemingly impossible things will become a reality. Our bodies will be healed, our minds renewed, our spirits revived, and our hearts made whole. We will see anew, feel differently, relate in an improved fashion. We will be healthy, wealthy, and wise—in all the things that truly matter. Such uncovering of mortal constraints and removal of cultural blind-spots requires divine help. The God of heaven can roll back the veil so that we may see that which is hidden from view. He can open our eyes, hearts, minds, spirits, and bodies to things we did not know and could not know without His unveiling intervention.

Unlock the Deep Potential Within Ourselves and Others

I have pondered much on the spiritual teaching that we are the children of God, created in His divine image and likeness. What does it mean for us to be created in the image and likeness of God? It means many things in restored doctrine taught by the Prophet Joseph Smith and his successors. Our likeness to God applies both spiritually and temporally. This profound truth conveys the idea that we are literally the spirit children of the Supreme Being. We are therefore endowed with capacities that are divine in nature. Our ability to reason, choose, love, serve, plan, forgive, create, and endure are just some of the attributes that mirror God's marvelous greatness. We are designed with intelligence, potential, gifts, and capabilities that reflect His ultimate light, His perfect knowledge, His amazing love, and His pure power. We possess profound latent potential. There is a spark of divinity within us. Our spirits are capable of holy experience such as receiving messages from God, feeling deep awe and wonder, having desires for nobility, gravitating toward the light of truth, and sensing profound joy.

Also, our similarity to God is not only a spiritual one. The First Vision itself bears profound witness that mortal men and women are in the literal likeness of God. Even our mortal bodies look like the Supreme Being and resemble His nature and characteristics to a certain extent. Joseph did not see aliens in the grove—he saw holy men of exalted glory. He was not visited by cosmic forces or beings of artificial intelligence. We have eyes to see like God has. We have ears to hear like God has. We have hands and feet like the Supreme Being has. The notion that our mortal bodies are created in the form and likeness of the Almighty is a stunningly powerful insight. We look like God! I believe that this provides tangible evidence that God lives. We could hardly be fashioned in the image of someone who does not exist! We display something of His grandeur. We are living witnesses of His reality. Our mortal body is a temple of divinity in that it is divinely designed. It is no small thing to be fashioned after the ultimate being.

All the incredible things that humans can do—such as remarkable gymnastic feats, memorizing thousands of words to recall them in many fresh and distinctive ways, playing the strategic game of chess, orchestrating complex musical symphonies, designing space rockets, and a thousand other things—are proof to my heart and soul of our being endowed with intelligence originating from God. I note that all of these abilities bless more than the person who performs them. They are a gift to others!

In this life, we can also be spiritually born again. We can become sons and daughters of Jesus Christ through holy ordinances and sacred covenants (see Mosiah 5). Thus, we become partakers of the divine nature and obtain the mind of Christ while still living in mortality.

This is impressive to me, and it is encouraging and empowering. We actually receive the image of Christ in our countenance (see Alma 5). This is further evidence that God lives because we are continually remade again and again in His image and likeness. Being born again to a newness of life is real. I am grateful that it has been happening to me. This process unlocks a potential within us that can be brought forth in no other way.

Further, we know that in the eternities, we will take upon us a body that will never again die. All resurrected beings are blessed with immortality. If we choose to live after the manner of God, we will be blessed with a glorious body in the Resurrection. This is a continuation and expansion of the way of righteousness as the essential pattern of our mortal lives. This blessing is better than having a mortal body because it is a qualitative improvement over mortality and it lasts eternally, unlike mortality (see Alma 40–42). This sublime gift will make us further like the God we worship.

The simple and profound truth is that every beautiful idea, every kind tendency, every wonderful word, every act of courage, and all good things in life bear testimony of the reality of the fatherhood of God and the truth that we are His offspring, His treasures, His loved ones. He is feeling after us, watching over us, guiding us, and preparing us for a glory beyond description. Every word of God that causes us to bow in humility before His royal nature and tremendous character is evidence that God is at work in this world. Lovely art, sublime music, and heavenly literature inspire us to look to Him as the perfect Father.

Let us remember who we truly are, whose we are, and who we can become. We are children of glory, sons and daughters of destiny, and inheritors of a precious promise that God is good and intends to work with us to help us become more than what we now are. We can look in the mirror, open our eyes, open our hearts, come to ourselves, and see the deep reality of these sobering things. We are children in God's image and likeness with the opportunity to become all that He designs for us to become—fully mature grown adults with everlasting perfection within us.

I believe we are giving ourselves a gift when we see ourselves in this divine light. We will live differently when we know we are divine. I also believe that we bestow a gift upon God when we see ourselves as His children. This is because we give Him the gift of what we do with our lives when we know He is the source of our souls. I further believe that we give others a gift when we see them as children of God. This is due to the truth that we will call forth the light within them when we view them as divinely precious. Hence, great gifts arise from us acknowledging and believing the light and truth we receive from God.

Envision Eternal Opportunities to Love

We do not learn to serve in this life simply to stop serving after death. We are preparing now for those things that are yet to come. There are yet greater opportunities that lie before us in the eternities for the full use of our talents, gifts, and abilities. We are born to love, and we are born again to love more deeply.

When this earth is made celestial, it will be because it is a place of creative fullness: "For after it hath filled the measure of its creation, it shall be crowned with glory, even with the presence of God the Father; . . . And again, verily I say unto you, the earth abideth the law of a celestial kingdom, *for it filleth the measure of its creation*, and transgresseth not the law" (Doctrine and Covenants 88:19, 25; emphasis added).

This earth keeps the law of abundance, the doctrine of multiplication. It teems with life. It abounds with beauty. It does not squander its opportunities. It lives to the full extent possible in both quantity and quality. Due to this compliance with creative law, the earth will receive the blessing of God's immediate presence. It will know eternal productivity. The life hereon will be long and glorious for all forms of life.

In a similar way, those privileged to abide on this earth in the fullness of its glory will be partakers of eternal creativity, continuous productivity, everlasting glory, and unending opportunity. Those opportunities will be ones of love, joy, and increase. If we are givers of good gifts in this life, then we will be givers of good gifts in the eternities to come.

Develop an Unending Faith, Hope, and Charity

Our faith in God is bound up with eternity. Our religion is one of creative enterprise. It is concerned with doing God's work for time and all eternity. To believe in God is not a temporary thing. To live righteously is not simply for a season. To share in the principles of truth is an ongoing project. We are to carry our knowledge of things divine inside of us through life everlasting. There is no end to the good that comes from being good. There is no dissolution of our confidence in eternal law. There is no retraction of our most abundant convictions. Rather, God will take our beliefs and magnify them, multiply them, refine them, perfect them, and bring them to full fruition. Our connection with God is a union that never fades. Rather, it expands. Improvement, progression, and enhancement are God's bestowal upon those who have determined to choose the right as an everlasting inheritance.

I call to mind again that the revelations say that "eye hath not seen, nor ear heard, neither have entered into the heart of man, the things which God has prepared for them that love him" (1 Corinthians 2:9). I believe this promise. We do not fully comprehend the rewards of our faith in Jesus Christ. We have not yet considered in full what lies ahead of us. We do not have the capacity, as mortal beings, to understand things from God's vantage point. His promise is to stun us, to amaze us, to shock us. This means that the sights we see, words we hear, and feelings we feel will be beyond what we can envision now. Eternity is not just forever. It is also qualitatively superb. It is an experience beyond compare. Surely, this means not only the opportunities for our growth and development; it also means relationships will be better, brighter, and more heavenly. I hope in all these greater things to come.

Our love for God does not fade into the background when we die. Our identity does not disappear. Our knowledge does not vanish away. Our memories are not erased. We remember with more vividness, we love with more intensity, we share with more eagerness, we bless with more generosity, we care with more empathy. We are in many ways now a preparatory shadow of what we will be then. We are an echo. We are limited, curtailed, kept back. In the forever world, we will know freedom to learn, discover, invent, create, and rejoice that we can only long for now. The scales of blindness will be removed, the concern with small things will vanish, and the lack of understanding will be gone. Our confusion will turn to clarity. Our ignorance will be replaced with knowledge. Our density will give way to comprehension. Our misgivings will yield to rejoicing. Our sorrows will bend to happiness. If we can catch even a partial vision now of what lies ahead of us in God's eternity, then we will be empowered to endure, serve, love, and bless in greatly magnified ways. Let us keep eternal things at the forefront of our minds and hearts. In due course, we will be astonished because of joy, overwhelmed with tears, and fall to our knees with soaring gratitude for the perfect goodness of God.

Live in One Eternal Family Round

The idea of family is a powerful one. I think of it as a link joining the great chain of God's family together. Family is not intended to be temporary. It is part of the "one eternal round" (Doctrine and Covenants 3:2) that God has in mind for His children. A round is that which signifies wholeness, timelessness, endlessness, perfection, unity, and singularity. For example, friendship, engagement, and wedding rings are round. This is intentional as it signifies the enduring nature of the relationship. This is one reason why wedding rings have come to symbolize so ideally the union of spouses.

The origin of the tradition of wedding rings is that ancient Egyptians believed that the ring finger, or the fourth finger of the left hand, contained a *vena amoris*, or "vein of love," that led directly to the heart. The Romans adopted this belief and wore wedding rings on their ring finger. Wedding rings have practical, symbolic, and sentimental value. The ring is usually made of a precious metal—such as gold or silver—and thus resembles the special, rare, and precious nature of the love between the parties. The precious metals show that your love is your most precious possession. It is to be valued highly and treated with respect.

Rings are usually circular, a shape that has a universal, centuries-old meaning representing notions of eternity, infinity, timelessness, and wholeness. It has implications of being unbroken and unbreakable. The circular shape indicates its meaning of being without beginning and without end. Thus, it has become a recognizable sign of eternal love, faithfulness, perfection, and endlessness.

Wedding rings exchanged between a man and woman signify:

- Eternity—it is an outward sign of an inward and spiritual bond that unites two hearts in endless love
- The unbreakable bond of lifelong love, devotion, and commitment between two married people—the strong union is intended to continue even through difficulty
- The sharing of wealth, status, family, and friendship between the two persons
- The swearing of an oath of fidelity and perpetual allegiance to a spouse
- A reminder to one and all that someone is married and is not available for any romantic relationship with another person

The giving of wedding rings represents the vows and promises the bride and groom have exchanged. They signify to the world that they belong to someone special and that someone special belongs to them. To give your spouse a ring signifies your never-ending love, devotion, and the joining of two families. It is a constant reminder of you stating to one another, "I love you," "I wish to be with you forever," "You are mine," and "I am yours."

The following words spoken during ring exchanges indicate that the giving of the ring represents the mutual sharing of love:

- "I give you this ring as a symbol of my everlasting love for you."

- "I give you this ring as a sign of our love for and commitment to each other. I promise to support you, care for you, and stand alongside you for all our days."
- "I offer you this ring to wear as a symbol of our unbreakable bond."

There is great emotional importance attached to wedding rings. All of this indicates why rings are such an important part of married life. It also explains why many people wear their rings constantly, why they might be frantically worried when they damage or lose them, and why they might keep them even when their spouse passes away. The ring is a tangible reminder of the person who is loved.

From a doctrinal point of view, eternal marriage is intended to be an everlasting covenant. Obviously, the full perfection we seek can only come in covenant union with God and our spouse. Clearly, the full measure of this perfection resides only in eternal glory. Marriages that are celestial in nature bring to fruition the full possibility of our divine nature. Both the man and the woman are made perfect in and through covenant union through God. To be perfect in this sense is to be eternally joined with God and our spouses in a perfect arrangement. There is no death of any kind in such a union. There is no sin in such an arrangement. There is no weakness, no imperfection, no lack, and no limitation in this heavenly partnership. It is an unbroken and unbreakable union.

Modern revelation unites with ancient revelation to give us an understanding of the temporal and spiritual alignment of the great sealing power of the priesthood. The seal cannot be broken once it is forged eternally. In the glory of celestial Resurrection, both spirit and body are united in harmony (see Doctrine and Covenants 88; 93; 132). The enemies of marriage and family no longer have power to afflict, tempt, denigrate, or destroy. In addition, the full flowering of character comes only then. In essence, eternal marriage is more grand and glorious than even the best of earthly marriages can be.

When we endeavor to envision our eternal family a million years from now and the great blessings that will be upon our families then, this acts as an encouragement to us now. Can we do anything more than merely glimpse the blissful nature of eternal family opportunities? The element of fulfillment, the sense of satisfaction, the feeling of serenity, the recognition of peace, the measure of accomplishment—these are the things that will come upon us to degrees not presently grasped in their fullness when we consider what the eternal measure of an exalted family represents. I believe we give a gift of eternal duration and worth when we bind ourselves to God and family in this special way.

Return Our Talents to God with an Increase

I often think of the parable of the talents. We usually consider the gifts given to us so that we might magnify them so the Lord has accrued interest when He returns. Hence, if we have one gift, the Lord expects us to double it. If we are given two gifts, we should find a way to make them into four. If we have five gifts, we need to turn them into ten. This is a perfectly appropriate way to think about the meaning the Lord had in mind. But another way we can think about this parable is to imagine that the talents represent people we are responsible to shepherd back to Him:

- If we are given "one" talent—let's say a spouse, for example—then we are expected to bring that person to the Lord in addition to ourselves. Is that not a doubling of our gift?
- If we are given "two" talents—like being given a spouse and one child—then we are expected to bring those two persons to the Lord *and* two others. The two others we might be expected to bring to the Lord are our child's eventual spouse and his or her children. Is that not a worthy portion of "interest" on our talents?
- If we are given "five" talents—such as being given a spouse and four children—then we are expected to bring those five persons to the Lord and the extended family of our children to the Lord. Is that not a very worthy offering to the Lord?

This interpretation of the parable fits in nicely with the idea of the Abrahamic covenant. Abraham wanted to be a father of the faithful. He desired to bring souls to the Lord. In the first instance, that meant his own family—his father, his wives, and his children. He wanted to bring Isaac to the Lord. In this way of looking at the parable of the talents, it makes sense that Abraham was willing to offer Isaac to the Lord—Isaac was the gift/talent/soul that Abraham was willing to freely give to the Lord (see Doctrine and Covenants 132:29–37).

In this sense, we are bringing souls to the Lord, not just talents and resources. It is people who are most important to the Lord. We could apply this principle to friends and acquaintances also. If we only ever have two friends, we can invite them to come to the Lord. We can also invite them to each bring a friend to the Lord. In this way, we are bringing four people to the Lord in addition to ourselves. Surely this would please the Lord. Surely our gifts to speak, preach, lead, bless, administer, organize, serve, and so on are really given to us so that we might bring souls to Christ. That is the great purpose of gifts, talents, abilities, and resources. The Lord already has land, money, and property. What He wants is people's souls. He wants His brothers and sisters to find salvation in Him. I believe this is the main reason we are given spiritual gifts and indeed all gifts from God. It is not just for the great blessing of the gifts themselves. It is for the purpose of bringing souls to rejoice in Christ.

This also explains why the Lord was so unhappy with the first servant who hid his talent in the field. In other words, he kept his "person" away from the Lord. He did not bring his spouse, on this possible interpretation, to the Lord. He kept her away from God. He did not perform his sacred stewardship as a husband and father in the way he should have. His talent (spouse) was taken from him and given to the man who had ten (see Doctrine and Covenants 132:38–39). This also indicates why the Lord was so happy with the second servant who brought his two talents to the Lord and two other talents also—he brought four souls to God! The third servant brought his five doubled talents to the Lord—he brought himself *and* ten other people to God!

I believe that the Lord rejoices when we seek earnestly to bring our families to God. What gift could be of more import?

Of course, we can seek to bring many souls to God, including friends, strangers, and even enemies! This will greatly please our Savior! I am profoundly grateful that we are gift-giving and gift-receiving people. Gifts—whether small or large, material or intangible, frequent or irregular—are a great and pointed reminder that we are not forgotten. They are also a clear opportunity for us to showcase our remembrance of and affection for others. We have gifts to give. We have a role to play in the lives of others. We have unique contributions to make to the souls placed in our path. It is an eternal work to seek to share our gifts with others in appropriate and sensitive ways. Who knows what good we might accomplish by sharing something precious of ourselves with others!

Forge Everlasting Friendships

The truest friend is one who helps us look toward the light, who hears our sorrows, who comforts our soul, who encourages our nobler nature, and who promotes our greatest interest. To have a true friend is wonderful. To be a good friend is indeed commendable. Our friendships now are but a token of that which is to come. They are a sign of that which is greater. They are the portion but not the whole. They point to that which is even more sublime, more sacred, more complete.

The gospel cause is the greatest friendship we can know. It is a union of divine purpose. It is a great fellowship of nobility. It is edifying and uplifting. To be bound in truth and righteousness with others whose motives are the same as ours is a tremendous blessing. Perfection in our friendships is a blessing of God. It is the call to the greatest circle of friends. It is the invitation to the most wonderful of all brotherly and sisterly connections. It is an opportunity to engage in the associations that never get derailed by worldly concerns or by broken promises. It is the union of true brotherhood and sisterhood in God.

Christ makes people great, and He makes their friendships great. He makes their word their bond, their natures loyal, their promises important, their devotions sacred. It is the Son of God who saves men and women, who unites people, who ties friends in everlasting communion. Our Savior brings people up from the grave and overcomes their iniquities. He banishes our pettiness, our rivalry, our one-upmanship, our conflicts. He turns us to forgiveness, to peace-making, to compassion. He makes us new, better, stronger, wiser.

Prepare Now for the Most Blissful Relationships Ever

Let us consider the times when our relationships have been at their most beautiful. These golden moments are like being wrapped inside a bubble of joy. The sense of connection and peace is almost palpable. These are times when we feel the goodness of genuine love—that mutual regard and concern that moves far beyond selfishness, pride, or lust, where we see and are seen, know and are known. The gospel of God is intended not simply to perfect individuals. It is also intended to make relationships whole, complete, and full. I believe that only when the veil is drawn back, only when the limitations of our fallen nature are removed, and only when we embrace the finest aspects of our divine nature will we know the fullness of bliss associated with eternal relationships grounded in true and pure love. Take the most wonderful relationships you have ever had in this frail world and imagine them refined, polished, and greatly magnified—that is what awaits us in the eternal glory that lies beyond this mortal time. We will only comprehend these blissful belongings properly when we experience them. Our gift of being friends to God and our fellow man can be an everlasting one.

17

BECOME PERFECT IN CHRIST

FINALLY, LET US DISCUSS THE ULTIMATE PERFECTION THAT WE SEEK in Christ. Human perfection may seem like an impossible dream. We can come up with convincing arguments for why such a state is beyond the capability of mortals. And we would be correct. Mortals cannot become perfect on their own. We need divine help. Our Savior not only makes such perfection possible—He makes it inevitable. What is required of us it to unite ourselves with Him in covenant connection and abide with Him always. He will make us more than we could ever be without Him.

Through loyal linking with our Lord via ordinances and covenants, we will become:

- **Alive** *in* Christ (see Moroni 8:12). To become "alive in Christ" is greatly needed in our day and age. This newness of life gives us an astonishing, distinctive, revelation-based connection to the Son of God. It awakens our soul to new thoughts, profound feelings, majestic ideas, deep discoveries, enhanced relationships, revised plans, and remarkable promises. This is an emergence to a different kind, type, and degree of life, both in time and eternity. The Savior has the power to impact our total self with amazing, renewing, and revitalizing capacity.

- **Cultivated** *in* Christ. This is the process of growth, development, and refinement that comes when we accept Christ's offer to us of a higher and holier kind of life.
- **Perfected** *in* Christ (see Moroni 10:32). This is what we become and can offer to the world when we come unto Christ with serious intent. We are made whole in and through the Son of God, not through our own efforts alone. We also become *sanctified* in Christ and *holy* in Christ (see Moroni 10:33). This happens through the grace of Christ on the condition that we love and serve God with all our might, mind, and strength (see Doctrine and Covenants 20:31).

I have at times felt like a bird wading through quicksand or mud. I have sometimes felt weighed down, heavy, stuck to the ground. I have felt that I am supposed to be flying, soaring, and feeling light. Instead, I can't seem to lift off. I am earthbound, tied, chained, prohibited. It is like being in a dream where you need to escape an enemy, but you can neither run nor even walk very fast. I have felt held back, curtailed, limited. Even when the bird gets out of the mud or quicksand, there is still the material that holds on, that adheres itself to your wings. The sense is one of being dragged down, anchored, held hostage.

I have many times felt like the world was clutching me, snatching me, grasping me, clinging to me. It does not want to let go. The world is like a bad memory you are trying to forget but can't seem to, or a so-called friend who leads you down dark paths and keeps visiting you even after you said you want to move on, or a trauma that hurt you badly and keeps resurfacing just when you think you are free from its tentacles. The world seems so earthy, so insistent, so reluctant to bid you farewell. It is conniving in that it seeks to seduce you to remain a prisoner to its insidious ways.

Have you ever felt like this? I believe every one of us has. We each have some element of weakness, limitation, shortcoming. This temporal fallen world allows temptation to abound everywhere. It seems that the tendency for carnality is easy to incline toward. Envy, lust, pride, greed, sloth, gluttony, and wrath—often referred to as the seven deadly sins—seem to appear in manifest forms through nearly all cultures and time periods. Every accountable person can relate to each one of these. They almost seem to be written into the very DNA of mortal life.

Can we even conceive of a world where the following dangerous and deadly proclivities did not exist?

- The desire to obtain things that belong to others
- The tendency to use others as instruments of our gratification
- The feelings of animosity for others
- The wanting of something at the expense of others
- The idling away of our time and opportunities
- The consumption of too many unhealthy substances
- The losing of our tempers with others

Can we imagine being able to transcend these desires ourselves? While it may seem folly to suggest that such traits can ever be overcome, the restored gospel of Jesus Christ is the divine pattern for teaching us that such is both possible and commendable. We are not bound down to the limitations of mortal patterns of thought only. We are not restricted to the opinions of those who do not see through the lens of gospel understanding. God's message is that He can and will change our very nature at the most fundamental level if we let Him work within us. Not only can these negative characteristics be reduced, but they can be replaced by their direct opposites. In their place we can develop generosity, virtue, humility, temperance, persistence, moderation, and love. These traits will be Christ-made ones. Further, we can become wholly, fully, completely, and entirely like Christ in the full measure of these personal attributes. That is stunning, true, and powerful doctrine.

I now discuss the perfection of the Son of God and how He will make us like Him. In this process, we can come to offer Him that which He offers us—everything we have and are. There will be no holding back, no resentment, no reluctance. There will be a willingness to do what He would do, say what He would say, think what He would think, go where He would go, and know what He would know. This is the process of perfection. It is not an errand of fools, an idle dream, or a fable for children. It is a sacred promise. I believe the Savior can only give us what He is if we are willing to give Him all we are. This is not easy or automatic. It is grueling. It is serious. It is also richly beautiful and deeply inspiring.

Ponder the Perfection of Jesus Christ

When we consider the perfection of Christ, we mean that there is nothing left undone about His character. We are referring to His being complete, whole, finished, polished. He is not lacking in some fundamental way. Whether spiritually, intellectually, physically, or emotionally, He is in possession of all the attributes of perfection. This was not a condition He arrived at instantaneously. His was a long road of sustained effort and gradual growth.

What manner of man is this Christ of which we speak? He is the perfect man, the ultimate hero. He stands against the worst floods of wickedness and the strongest armies of darkness. The legacy of His life consisted of every choice He made, the details of His divinity, the temptations He resisted, the service He rendered, the miracles He performed, the character He evidenced, the atoning sacrifice He accomplished, and the Resurrection He made possible for all. His ministry is the sublime testament to His superb greatness. What kind of person was He? He was:

- A man of faith and hope (see Doctrine and Covenants 137:2)
- A man of prayer, scripture study, and exact obedience (see Alma 57:21; Doctrine and Covenants 136:42)
- A man of purity, having both clean hands and a pure heart (see Psalms 24:3–4)
- A man of peace (see Doctrine and Covenants 136:23–24)
- A man of covenant loyalty who submitted to righteous priesthood authority in receiving ordinances (see Doctrine and Covenants 136:4)

- A man who sought His Father's revelation and counsel (see Doctrine and Covenants 88:63; 136:19; Articles of Faith 1:9)
- A man who relied on the strength of His Father (see Doctrine and Covenants 136:32)
- A man who grew in difficult conditions and endured extreme testing well (see Alma 32; Doctrine and Covenants 136:31)
- A man of temple worship and service (see Doctrine and Covenants 137:8)
- A man of tremendous influence—a watchful shepherd, attentive healer, gentle lifter, merciful teacher, and leader who was slow to anger (see Doctrine and Covenants 136:10)

Christ is the great Master of righteousness, having achieved the ultimate perfection possible (see 3 Nephi 12:48). We are His apprentices. We are to become as He already is. This requires a mighty change of heart, a deep change in nature, a transformation in outlook, a shift in behavior, and a total reformation from sinner to saint. We are to walk in the way of the sublime Son. As the perfect man, He is all we aspire to be. He is the true exemplar, and we can seek to follow Him, learn of Him, and become more like Him. He lives. He loves. He lifts. He is eager for us to go where He is now. We are to see His image and likeness in the mirror when we look at it. Our appearance, actions, character, and substance are to reflect His marvelous goodness (see Alma 5:14, 26). Our countenance is to be like His.

His coming into the world is more important than anything else we could come to know about (see Alma 7:7). The knowledge of Him, not just intellectual or historical but experiential and personal, should move us to a new life individually. It also inspires us to share His good news with others so that they might rejoice. What do we think, feel, and know of Him? What do we love about Him? What love do we have for Him? Who is He really? He is our guide to holiness.

He walked the strait and narrow path in premortality, mortality, and post-mortality. He is the Atoning One, the Expiator, the Reconciler, the Propitiator, the Mediator. He took upon Himself the expedient burden of sin and death. His Father required much from

Him, and He gave His all to that onerous task. He gave Himself, with nothing held back. He suffered every kind and degree of difficulty—whether emotional, spiritual, social, mental, or physical. He experienced the toothaches, the vertigo, the strokes, the heart attacks, the cancer, the paralysis, and all other types of physical ailment that have been known in this world. He has taken upon Himself pains, sickness, death, and infirmities to comprehend our position precisely and intimately. He has power to blot out our transgressions.

He has known the greatest fear, the deepest loneliness, the ultimate sorrow, the most vicious anger, the deadliest vice, the worst treachery. He has known what it is to be abandoned, abused, divorced, ignored, bullied, and cast away. He has felt the loss, understood the grief, comprehended the misery, experienced the despair, and sensed the rejection associated with this fallen world, this wilderness of sin, this bleak domain. However, He has conquered, risen above, and been triumphant. He has overcome the lowest low, the deepest depth, and the most terrifying tragedy. He is mighty to save and to cleanse us from all unrighteousness, all bickering, all deceit, all lust, all arrogance, all procrastination, and all dread. Think of His victory. Think on His goodness. Reflect on His achievement. Consider His astounding offering to us!

Embrace the Concept of Perfection

The scriptures speak plainly about the expectations God has for us:

- Enoch walked with God (see Genesis 5:21–24).
- Noah was a *perfect* man who walked with God (see Genesis 6:9).
- Melchizedek was a great high priest (see Alma 13). He was so faithful and respected as an example of what a high priest should be like that the higher priesthood was called the Melchizedek Priesthood.

- Jehovah appeared to Abram (Abraham) when he was ninety years of age and said, "Walk before me, and be thou *perfect*" (Genesis 17:1; emphasis added).
- Moses was the *most meek* man on the earth (see Numbers 12:3).
- Job was *perfect* and walked uprightly before God (see Job 1:1).

This is not intended to indicate that these brethren were without flaw, mistake, or weakness throughout mortality. It does not mean they never committed any sin, error, or wrong. Nor were they finished in the work of perfection. They were not resurrected when the words of God were given to them. Nor were they free from the trials and tribulations of mortality (until they were lifted up to heaven, that is). They were still subject to aging, disease, and decay. They were still living in a fallen world where violence and immorality abounded. Nor did they know all things or have all power. They did not yet possess the fullness of character perfection.

However, it does indicate a high degree of internal spiritual consistency. They acted in accordance with what they knew. They wanted to do and be good. They achieved significant growth, mastery, and maturation in spiritual things because of intentional choices and diligent effort. They relied on God for help. They learned the laws of the Lord and tried sincerely to incorporate such into their lives. This was obviously not an easy, automatic, or stress-free process. It did not happen in a moment. It required time, significant work, and patient endurance.

The idea of perfection is not intended to leave us in a state of perpetual discontent. It is not expected that we constantly scrutinize every minute aspect of our behavior to be paralyzed into inaction. Of course, we all have fears, and we all have moments of great nervousness. We all think about whether we can possibly live up to the expectations placed upon us. These are all part of the human condition.

God wants to encourage us onward, not stifle us into inactivity. We sometimes give up on things because we dread the expectation that comes with having to perform at a high level. However, as we draw close to God, the tendency to be stunted due to fear gives way to a confidence that God is with us. He is far more interested in genuine trying and dogged persistence than He is in flawless performance.

I think of perfection as requiring two elements—first, the removal of that which holds us bound to weakness, and second, the incorporation of positive benefits into our lives. Hence, it involves not merely the removal of spiritual weakness but also the acquisition of strength and righteousness.

Think about what the removal of physical, mental, spiritual, and emotional limitations associated with mortality might mean:

- Clearing of mental fog
- Lifting of disability
- Removal of emotional hang-ups
- Overcoming of spiritual deficiencies
- Abandoning of misjudgments
- Clearing away of stereotypes
- Abandoning of cultural limitations
- Changing of reputations
- Breaking barriers of faulty thinking

Let us consider the example of Captain Moroni, the mighty man of Christ (see Alma 48:17). Mormon said that Captain Moroni was a man who yielded his heart to God willingly and genuinely. He reached the point of spiritual development where the adversary's attempts to entice him were futile. It is therefore possible to learn to resist temptation. We can school our feelings, educate our motives, rein in our aspirations, and control our thoughts. It is both true and faith-promoting to know that each of us can come off conqueror in the great battles of the soul that are waged inside of us. By doing this, we can become renewed in stunning righteousness. By this submission, we can gain all victory.

Believe That Christ Can Perfect Our Character

The glorious doctrine is that human weakness can be replaced with divine strength as we come to Christ with serious intent (see Ether 12:27):

- An attribute of fear can change to one of tremendous courage.
- A leaning of doubt can become a tendency toward great faith.
- A disposition of lust can give way to a state of mighty virtue.
- A characteristic of selfishness can yield to profound selflessness.
- A failing of laziness can bow to a disposition to hard work.
- A weakness of anger can be overcome by a strong and deep love.
- The dreaded disease of pride can be replaced by towering humility.

In fact, every human foible can be jettisoned, and instead there will come divine attributes and a godly nature through our deliberate coming to Christ. Such is the sure and certain promise of the revealed word. As we strive to emulate the character of Christ, we encourage others to do likewise. They are drawn to His perfect character.

Accept That Christ Perfects Our Knowledge and Understanding

Jesus Christ was a scriptorian in the best sense of that word. He knew the law and the prophets. He was familiar with doctrine, acquainted with prophecy, and aware of spiritual history. He was able to teach the words of scripture with powerful clarity and also capable of adding to, expanding, refining, correcting, and improving existing scripture. Christ is a teacher of truth, a preacher of righteousness. He wants us to learn the doctrine and teach it to others.

Our prophets are likewise men who seek a sound understanding of the revealed word. The Book of Mormon provides this useful insight into Alma and the sons of Mosiah:

Now these sons of Mosiah were with Alma at the time the angel first appeared unto him; therefore Alma did rejoice exceedingly to see his brethren; and what added more to his joy, they were still his brethren in the Lord; yea, and they had waxed strong in the knowledge of the truth; for they were men of a sound understanding and they had searched the scriptures diligently, that they might know the word of God.

But this is not all; they had given themselves to much prayer, and fasting; therefore they had the spirit of prophecy, and the spirit of revelation, and when they taught, they taught with power and authority of God. (Alma 17:2–3)

Hence, their knowledge of God's doctrine was not superficial. They had made substantial efforts to know scriptural truth, they had a proper understanding of God's word, and they were therefore deeply grounded in the principles of true religion. Of course, this was not simply a search for intellectual comprehension. Their regular communication with God through prayer and their spiritual discipline of the body was shown in much fasting. Therefore, power, prophecy and revelation attended their teaching. Thus, they were trying to mirror their Lord who was sublimely blessed with these abilities to a profound degree. Their acquired gifts were an invaluable support to others!

Our living prophets likewise have treasures of doctrine to share with us. President Nelson speaks to the Saints regularly about pristine truth, the clear doctrine of Christ, and the need for pure revelation. We are to sense these in their undiluted and unpolluted form. Each one of us can similarly come to know divine truth and receive inspiration to guide us personally. As we come to plain truth in Christ, we find unity in righteousness—the kind of harmony that is based on everlasting reality. This is how we as individuals gain a secure spiritual footing. It is also how the world can overcome division, contention, and animosity that arises from not knowing or not heeding the doctrine of Christ. Unity must be in Christ for salvation. It ultimately is based on knowing, believing, and living the revealed word of God. As we come to doctrinal unity with Christ, we inspire others to do likewise. Indeed, they will gravitate toward His perspective on the truths of eternity. It will be like a magnet to their souls!

See That Christ Perfects Our Access to Light

Christ is the embodiment of light. He personifies light. He radiates it. He is a being of marked luminosity, clear brightness, and transparent illumination. This signifies His knowledge, information, understanding, and enlightenment. It also evidences His intelligent goodness. His comprehension is not just of the mind—it is also of the spirit. He is the power by which we see. He is good enough to share His light with us. He does not want us to remain in dark corners, shady places, or locations of despair. He wants to bring us into the light, to sense His light, to know His glory, and to partake of His intelligence. He wants us to become beings of light like He is. In His perfect light, we find a fullness of light. We are made vessels of light as we come to spend time with Him, learn of Him, walk in His ways, and know of His glories. The light is to be bathed in, basked in, immersed in, and clothed in. His spiritual electricity will fill us with quickness, alertness, discernment, wisdom, judgment, and glowing. To walk in a fullness of light is to find Christ perfectly. As we come to His light, we seek to draw others to that light. In Him they find light that allows them to see!

Allow Christ to Perfect Our Peace

The rewards of discipleship are many. One of the great blessings that comes to us through the Son of God is peace of conscience, peace of mind, peace within. For example, one of the scriptural injunctions to the Saints is that they should stand fast in the Lord. This means that we are to be loyal to the Lord. This standing firm is to occur in the presence of difficulty, trouble, affliction, and opposition. Those challenges are to be regular. Hence, the Saints are to anticipate tribulation but are to remain committed to following the Savior. As a result of standing steadfast in that faith in Jesus Christ, the Saints are promised the blessing of divine peace: "And the peace of God, which passeth all understanding, shall keep your hearts and minds through Christ Jesus" (Philippians 4:7).

In essence, Saints are told that God's peace, which is beyond our capacity to comprehend unless and until we receive it, is bestowed upon our minds and hearts. This peace enable us to face every problem, keep our resolve though suffering, and retain the devotion to Christ that is so necessary for our mortal efforts and so essential to our eternal salvation. This peace does not make sense to outside observers. It seems irrational, illogical, and unfounded. How can we as Saints find peace when we are afflicted with so many trials? To the natural man, such peace is simply inexplicable. However, to those followers of Christ who endure the many whirlwinds of life in this world, the promises are not empty and hollow. Instead, they are sweet to the souls of those who partake of them.

In our day, the Lord has once again revealed His message from heaven. He has declared His treasures from the earth and heralded His glories from the skies. He has given us knowledge of His plan and purposes through a modern prophet, Joseph Smith. He has bestowed upon us priesthoods, powers, keys, privileges, gifts, and marvels. He has given us the glorious Comforter, the Holy Ghost. He has given us peace as we strive to be true to the good and holy works that He has called us to perform: "But learn that he who doeth the works of righteousness shall receive his reward, even peace in this world, and eternal life in the world to come" (Doctrine and Covenants 59:23)

This is the kind of heavenly peace that can be obtained even when the world is at war. The type of peace that prevails even when we are faced with illness, betrayal, heartbreak, loss, confusion, despair, and tragedy. We are not immune to hardship or deep struggle. We get sick, feel pain, know disappointment, experience anxiety, face worry, and are intimately acquainted with temptations of all kinds. In addition, we see these storms of sorrow face others we love, strangers we never meet in person, and even enemies who perhaps have hurt us. We see affliction come upon all people, families, and nations. None are immune.

However, the promises of God are sure. Christ is the Prince of Peace. The Comforter is the bringer of peace. Our Father in Heaven showers peace upon us in our times of greatest distress. This peace must be experienced to be properly understood. I have known this peace many times. Even when it rationally seemed like there was nothing to be at peace about, I have known of that contentment, that assurance, that confirmation that God is good and life in Him is sweet, even when the world is in turmoil. I have known comfort when sick, love when alone, relief when troubled, and joy when tormented. When I was afflicted by the world or by my own shortcomings or fears, I have nonetheless been sheltered and assured by the reality of God's watchful care. I am grateful beyond words to know that each one of us can come unto the God of Israel and feel that precious personal peace He longs to bestow upon us. We can also lead others to that perfect peace. In the peace of Christ, they will find rest.

Offer Our Whole Soul to Christ

The Lord invites us to make offerings in righteousness, in the name of Christ, by covenant and sacrifice, according to the desires of our hearts (see 3 Nephi 24:3; Doctrine and Covenants 132:9, 51; Joseph Smith—History 1:15). An offering to the Lord is to be the right offering, made with sincere feelings, made in the name of the Son of God, made in a spirit of promise, and made with the willingness to forego that which is "less than" in favor of that which is "more than." We are invited to give all that we have to our Father and His Son, with no holding back. It is the achievement of a lifetime if we can accomplish this genuine willingness. This means we are also to give all we have in blessing the lives of God's children. The great irony of life is that as we give all we have, we receive all that can be received. The greatest gift is bestowed upon the greatest giver!

Gift Our Sovereign Will to God

President Boyd K. Packer decided in his life to offer his moral agency to the Lord. He said that he essentially surrendered his agency to the Lord and by so doing became truly free. An *Ensign* article written around the time of his death made the following observation about that very personal offering to the Lord:

Many years ago, after receiving a personal witness on that tiny island in the Pacific, he wanted to give something back. He wanted to formalize his commitment as a disciple of Jesus Christ.

"It had become critically important," he remembered, "to establish this intention between me and the Lord so that I knew that He knew which way I had committed my agency. I went before Him and said, 'I'm not neutral, and you can do with me what you want. If you need my vote, it's there. I don't care what you do with me and you don't have to take anything from me because I give it to you—everything, all I own, all I am.'"

Those who loved and honored Boyd K. Packer will have every confidence that the Lord has accepted his offering, an offering magnified through a lifetime of sacred service.[10]

There is much to learn from this. I often think that we create extra hardship for ourselves because we struggle stubbornly against our Father in Heaven and our Savior. We often wish to do our own thing and reject their benevolent authority. We engage in a power struggle with them. Instead of doing this, we can choose to submit and use our agency to follow. Obviously, this is difficult. But it is also possible and beneficial. I find I rejoice far more when I submit to their teachings and love.

I have always been impressed by Elder Neal A. Maxwell, who also spoke about this theme of giving ourselves to God:

> In conclusion, the submission of one's will is really the only uniquely personal thing we have to place on God's altar. The many other things we "give," brothers and sisters, are actually the things He has already given or loaned to us. However, when you and I finally submit ourselves, by letting our individual wills be swallowed up in God's will, then we are really giving something to Him! It is the only possession which is truly ours to give! Consecration thus constitutes the only unconditional surrender which is also a total victory![11]

---

10. "In Memoriam: President Boyd K. Packer: Farewell to a Master Teacher," *Ensign*, Aug. 2015.
11. Neal A. Maxwell, "Swallowed Up in the Will of the Father," *Ensign*, Nov. 1995, 24.

I agree with these Apostles! Giving to God that which He will not take or force us to give is the greatest offering we can possibly make. I do not believe that ultimate perfection is possible without our willingness to adopt this position. Each of us needs to choose if we will make our peace with this request. I believe that coming to this point makes our perfection in Christ a truly joyful inevitability. There are blessings that come to us only on the condition that we offer our inner selves freely to God.

Choose to Follow God's Perfect Plan

The course of the Lord is one eternal round. Consider the words of God to Joseph Smith regarding the loss of the book of Lehi:

> The works, and the designs, and the purposes of God cannot be frustrated, neither can they come to naught.
>
> For God doth not walk in crooked paths, neither doth he turn to the right hand nor to the left, neither doth he vary from that which he hath said, therefore his paths are straight, and his course is one eternal round.
>
> Remember, remember that it is not the work of God that is frustrated, but the work of men. (Doctrine and Covenants 3:1–3)

This is a solemn and sobering declaration. God has a plan. He has a purpose. That majestic plan and grand purpose is not like a feather in the breeze. It is not like a ship in the storm. It does not become derailed because of the fragility, stubbornness, or short-sightedness of men. The God we worship is not engaged in subterfuge, trickery, or treachery. He is not shocked by the cunning of men or the designs of devils. He is not caught off guard. He cannot be outsmarted, outclassed, or outgunned.

God is an upright being, with honesty and goodness at the core of His actions. He does not have to come up with a plan B or a plan C to compensate for the evils of men. His doctrine is sure and sound. His strait and narrow path is not temporary in nature, nor is it subject to dismissal or alteration. Men can lose their way, forfeit their souls, betray friends, make colossal errors, and be stubborn and rebellious. Men can be deceived, tricked, and hoodwinked. They can lose their resolve. God falls into no such traps. His ways are eternal. His manner of living is an everlasting journey. His comings and goings are not arbitrary but clear and determined. His work to save is His ongoing work and glory. The loss of the book of Lehi could not and would not stop the work of God from progressing. Provision had been made.

In like manner, the perfection of God is not temporary. It is definitive and everlasting. The perfection He offers us is an eternal reward, not a temporary status. When we find salvation through God, our opportunity and privilege is to enjoy that benefit forever and to be eternally engaged in the work of salvation for others.

Partake in Christ's Last Will and Testament

As part of the process of deeding their property to their children in the form of a legal inheritance, parents create a last will and testament. They make solemn promise in a written record that they will bestow certain temporal rewards upon those they love. This legacy is a serious act. It is not to be trifled with. I think the holy scriptures and the spoken promises of the Lord perform a similar function in the spiritual realm. These scriptures are "testaments" in the sense of being testimonies, covenants, and witnesses of the Father and the Son. They announce the will and plans of the Lord, especially concerning God's children. We might call them a form of last will and testament as they pronounce the intended blessings of God for His faithful covenant children—those who are heirs to the birthright of blessings. We inherit all blessings from God if we obey His will and testament. The most exalting blessings—perfection in the blissful abodes above—only come through the deeding to us by the Father and Son of all spiritual endowments in time and eternity. As God the Father lives, He will bestow the pinnacle of perfection upon all those who seek it with all their souls through His Beloved Son.

Become Gifted in Christ

Our Savior seeks to bless us in every possible aspect of our lives. He makes us better. Indeed, He makes us the best we can ever be. Christ increases our spiritual might, enhances our intellectual capacity, improves our physical strength, and develops our emotional and social abilities. Indeed, He can bring all of these to a level where nothing is left lacking. That is as astonishing promise.

I know that we have personal gifts to offer to Him and others. These are offerings that are unique to us. They are special. The Father and Son rejoice when we offer our special love and lives to them and our fellow brothers and sisters. I encourage you to continue to pray for those gifts that you can then cultivate and offer to the glory of God and the blessing of His children. Such offerings will please the Lord because both we and others will be truly and richly blessed in this endeavor.

I offer humble testimony that Christ is in truth that chosen Messiah. I bear witness of His revealing Prophet Joseph. I know from experiences that I have had—some of which I have shared in my writing, and others which I cannot share because they are too sacred or because I do not have adequate words to express them—that Jesus is indeed the living Holy One. He is gifted with all heavenly gifts. He longs to share His gifts with us. As we partake of His gifts, we become truly gifted. We become able to rise and shine, to light the world, to strengthen the weak, to comfort the lonely, to inspire the hopeless, and to encourage the distraught. We develop and use gifts that are beautifully precious. Our offerings of these gifts to God and others will bring a joy to the world that otherwise could not exist. The whole souled excellence of body, mind, heart, and spirit that we find in Christ can also be ours. By, in, and through Him, we will find that we are made whole, complete, and finished. Perfection is a reality when we take Christ at His word. I love, honor, and sustain Him and commend Him to you without reservation.

My beloved brothers and sisters, I am grateful that my thoughts and feelings on the Lord Jesus Christ are written. I gratefully share my knowledge and testimony of Him. I am thankful to share my wondrous awe about the phenomenal newness of life that the Messiah offers to us, about the miracles that happen to us when we accept His offer, and about the great gifts we can offer Him and others through our covenant devotion to God in time and eternity. I hope that these supernal opportunities will remain with you and your loved ones as a perpetual legacy for a long time to come. Indeed, may joyful perfection in Christ be upon you and yours through the beautiful eternal round that awaits all who come to Christ with all their souls. So be it!

About the Author

THOMAS HOLTON LIVES IN IRELAND. HE HAS DEGREES FROM THREE Universities and certification in financial planning. He has tutored teenagers in English and Mathematics and coached business undergraduates in "writing for business" skills. He has also given training lectures on taxation. He has worked as an administrator and manager for twenty-four years.

His Church service includes being a missionary in England, temple ordinance worker, adult Sunday School teacher four times, ward mission leader twice, branch/district/stake Sunday School president, elders quorum president twice, branch Young Men president, membership of branch presidencies and bishoprics for fifteen years, stake high councilor, and Church history specialist for the island of Ireland. His health challenges over twenty-six years have taught him empathy and resilience.

He is the author of *Alive in Christ* and *Cultivated in Christ*. He and His wife, Veronica, are the grateful parents of one adult son.

Scan to visit

https://words-of-wonder.com/